MW01506321

Merry Chr...
Hope you enjoy
Love,
Alan
2008

A SEA OF CHANGE

A Sea of Change

Ernest Hemingway and the Gulf Stream

A Contextual Biography

MARK P. OTT

THE KENT STATE UNIVERSITY PRESS · KENT, OHIO

© 2008 by The Kent State University Press, Kent, Ohio 44242
ALL RIGHTS RESERVED
Library of Congress Catalog Card Number 2007044976
ISBN 978-0-87338-923-5
Manufactured in the United States of America

LIBRARY OF CONGRESS CATALOGING-IN-PUBLICATION DATA
Ott, Mark P., 1966–
A sea of change : Ernest Hemingway and the Gulf Stream :
a contextual biography / Mark P. Ott.
p.   cm.
Includes bibliographical references and index.
ISBN 978-0-87338-923-5 (hardcover : alk. paper) ∞
1. Hemingway, Ernest, 1899–1961—Criticism and interpretation.
2. Hemingway, Ernest, 1899–1961—Knowledge—Gulf Stream.
3. Hemingway, Ernest, 1899–1961—Knowledge—Natural history.
4. Hemingway, Ernest, 1899–1961—Homes and haunts.
5. Hemingway, Ernest, 1899–1961. To have and have not.
6. Hemingway, Ernest, 1899–1961. Old man and the sea.
7. Nature in literature.   I. Title.
PS3515.E37Z7515 2008
813'.52—dc22   2007044976

British Library Cataloging-in-Publication data are available.

12 11 10 09 08   5 4 3 2 1

Contents

I believe Ernest Hemingway was a lover of country, a patriot and a naturalist, at once, and I believe he was a deeply spiritual man in his attachment to place. Perhaps the pain he had to endure was in feeling too much. He had to create a mask to his own vulnerable nature. He could move. He could dodge. He could drink blood of Spanish bulls. But the memories of wild nature, the knowledge of wild nature, his need for wild nature never left him. That was his gulf stream, in his blood, on the land, on the page.

—TERRY TEMPEST WILLIAMS

Preface

Arriving at the Stream

IN THE LANGUAGE of geography, the Gulf Stream is a warm ocean current created by the flow of water from the Caribbean Sea through the Yucatan Channel between Mexico and Cuba. From there, it rushes through the Florida Keys into the seven hundred islands of the Bahamas, continuing along the eastern United States, and dissipating near Newfoundland. In the language of American studies, it is a "contested site": a place of Atlantic intercultural interaction between ethnic and racial groups joined in a community of water.

Within the canon of American literature, the Gulf Stream has long been an imaginary seascape in the minds of writers. James Fenimore Cooper, Richard Henry Dana, Herman Melville, Stephen Crane, and Ernest Hemingway all portrayed the Gulf Stream in their fiction. To the interpreters of these writers, the Gulf Stream functions as an extension of the frontier: it is the meeting point between savagery and civilization where America's providential mission affirmed itself. To African American writers such as Zora Neale Hurston, Paule Marshall, Jamaica Kincaid, Toni Morrison, and Charles Johnson, the Gulf Stream functions as a link to both Africa, through the Middle Passage, and Europe, through centuries of colonization. Yet to figures such as Derek Walcott, V. S. Naipaul, C. L. R. James, and Patrick Chamoiseau, a vaster universal compassion is required of the modern writer. The Gulf Stream acts as the point of intersection and blending of these creative traditions as writers with extraordinarily diverse talents, themes, and viewpoints create fiction portraying this region.

My initial project was to use the Gulf Stream as the unifying lens for a broad exploration of this fiction to create a text that investigated and appreciated the variations of the land and ocean encompassing the Caribbean and the Florida Keys. That work soon shifted to a more specific examination of how canonical American writers—Melville, Crane, and Hemingway—transformed and portrayed the region. Finally, my attention settled on the one writer I knew best: Hemingway.

The decision to focus on Hemingway was a natural one. After moving to Key West in 1928, Hemingway became increasingly enthralled with deep-sea fishing and the Gulf Stream. Of all the writers considered, he knew the Gulf Stream most intimately. As he understood more fully the daily life of the Stream, he became more integrated with it, less separate from it. Hemingway's relationship with the Gulf Stream evolved from one in which he experienced it as a space of conquest to a relationship that allowed him to understand it as a place of personal integration and harmony.

And, as a research project, he provided the most intriguing raw material. In the Ernest Hemingway Collection at the John F. Kennedy Library in Boston, I was able to read Hemingway's fishing logs from the years 1932, 1933, 1934, 1936, and 1939. Dense in the daily details of Hemingway's fishing excursions from Key West to Cuba and through the Bahamas, the logs had been surprisingly neglected by Hemingway scholars in the past. The more closely I read them, the more I became convinced of their significance as a tool to understanding Hemingway and the transformation of his work.

The logs record mundane details, such as the menu for lunch on July 30, 1934: "macaroni with meat, avacado [sic] salad, ham, fruit salad." The logs also contain the more intriguing details of catching a barracuda the next day: "Fish had hit so hard on a tight line that he was hooked in the gills. We noticed sepia black oozing from the wound the gaff made. Carlos opened him and in the belly found a small octopus freshly swallowed and a very large squid that had been sliced in two pieces." The economy and clarity of the description signal a shift in Hemingway's writing style, foreshadowing later work. For example, on May 17, 1932, Hemingway recorded:

hooked Marlin opposite
Cojimar 2 jumps threw hook—930
swam at beach 3pm—saw

first big striped marlin tail at least
three feet behind teaser deep down
—Back a foot or more across
came to surface and when we
curled boat but [illegible] down before
we saw baits (sky was very overcast) and had
strike from another marlin

Hemingway is trying to create a precise account of the moment, capturing objectively his observations through economical phrases—"big
striped marlin tail at least three feet"—in order to faithfully present
the ecosystem of the Cuban waters. Hemingway links the behavior of
the marlin with the overcast sky to understand their interdependence
in a way that foreshadows crucial elements of Santiago's narration. For
literally hundreds of pages in the fishing logs, Hemingway crafts short,
precise, representational descriptions of what he observed on the Gulf
Stream. He would of course use that knowledge later in his fiction. In
The Old Man and the Sea, Santiago is aware of what is beneath the surface of the ocean. He has studied the Gulf Stream, and he is aware of the
organic unity that exists within nature. In the fishing logs, Hemingway
is learning what exists beneath the iceberg.

Thus, the hypothesis is that the exact observations in the logs explain
the stylistic transformation—the shift in his writing method—that occurred in Hemingway's work between the publication of *A Farewell
to Arms* (1929) and *The Old Man and the Sea* (1952), a period during
which Hemingway moved from desiring to "write like Cezanne [*sic*]
painted" to wanting his books about the sea to contain illustrations by
Winslow Homer (Murphy, "Hemingway, Winslow Homer" 78).

. . .

Since I first conceived of this project, I have incurred many debts. When
I was a high school junior in 1983 at Madison LaFollette High School,
Susan Dean, now my friend and then my teacher, gave me a copy of
In Our Time, and my life has not been the same since. At the Univer-
sity of Wisconsin–Madison, Professors Richard Merelman and Thomas
Schaub inspired me to deepen my engagement with literature. At the
University of Wyoming, Eric Sandeen, John Dorst, and Lewis Dabney
provided moral and intellectual support, encouraging my burgeoning in-
terest in Hemingway. Later, at the University of Hawaii–Manoa, Floyd

Matson inspired me with his tales of lunching with Hemingway in 1941, and Joseph Stanton was unflagging in his support of this project since I first became enthused by affinities between Winslow Homer's work and Hemingway's depictions of the natural world in his seminar "The Sea in Art and Literature." His detailed comments and insights were exceptionally helpful. It would be impossible to overstate my debt to Professor David Stannard, my dissertation director; his suggestions and encouragement remain invaluable.

The Ernest Hemingway Society has provided substantial support for this project. I am grateful for the support of a James Hinkle Travel Grant and the Smith-Reynolds Fellowship. Indeed, this project draws from the knowledge of the scholars I have met through the Ernest Hemingway Society. I met Larry Grimes and Bickford Sylvester in Cuba in 1997, and since then I have benefited from their sage advice. Steve Paul and Robert Trogdon kindly shared their insights into the composition of *To Have and Have Not*, and Kirk Curnutt's comments on sections of my manuscript were also very beneficial. James Brasch very kindly answered questions about Hemingway's library. Scott Donaldson and Susan Beegel provided more encouragement than they realize, and Linda Miller, in her shared interest in Hemingway's fishing logs, has been generous in her support of my parallel scholarship. Gerald Kennedy facilitated permissions to publish sections of Hemingway's fishing logs; I am grateful for his assistance.

I have also received generous support from Tyler Tingley at Phillips Exeter Academy, John Gulla at the Blake School in Minneapolis, and Jim Scott at Punahou School in Honolulu. I am also grateful for the support of Margarita Curtis, John Taylor, and Mark Scandling of Deerfield Academy. Grants from the Arts and Sciences Advisory Council at the University of Hawaii–Manoa supported research trips, and the Graduate Student Organization provided funding for travel to conferences.

At the John F. Kennedy Library, Susan Wrynn, Meghan Desnoyers, James Roth, Stephen Plotkin, and Jennifer Wheeler have assisted in my research and allowed me to use photographs from the Hemingway Collection. I am especially grateful for an Ernest Hemingway Research Grant that supported two weeks of research in the Ernest Hemingway Collection. Gail Morchower and Doug Blodgett at the International Game Fishing Association Museum also provided very generous assistance. The staff of the Ewell Sale Stewart Library of the Academy of Natural Sciences also extended their services several times; to them I am grateful. Lydia Zelaya of Simon and Schuster assisted with acquiring permission to publish sections of Hemingway's fishing logs. I am also grateful to Sandra Wiskari of the Metropolitan Museum of Art for permission to use images of paintings by Paul Cézanne and Winslow Homer.

Most significantly, I want to thank Joanna Hildebrand Craig, Mary Young, and everyone at the Kent State University Press for their support of this project. Without Joanna's patience, skill, and sense of humor, this project could not have been completed, and Mary's editorial guidance was invaluable.

The advice and support of my friends have been essential. Harvard Knowles, Nita Pettigrew, Sean Melvin, Richard Raleigh, Michael Drummey, Rob Vaughan, David Zmijewski, John Cashman, and Michelle Dionne all kept me pushing forward in the midst of setbacks.

And then there is family: my parents, Daniel and Patricia Ott; Kathy and Matt Wehrli; Joe and Kris Ott; Greg and Lisa Ott; and the Ishimarus. Thanks.

And last, for the ever-patient Lori, Claire, and Anne: life will be different now that this is done.

CHAPTER I

The Sea Change Part I

The *Anita* Logs

AFTER MOVING TO Key West in 1928, Ernest Hemingway became increasingly enthralled with deep-sea fishing and the Gulf Stream. Hemingway had fished since he was a small boy; photos exist of a three-year-old Ernest, cane pole in hand, trying his luck off a dock in Petosky, Michigan. While fishing for trout in his twenties could be seen as a natural extension of his boyhood hobby, Hemingway's interest in saltwater fishing was completely different—more scientific than experiential, more ichthyologist than Huck Finn. Soon after his first fishing trip to Cuba in 1932, Hemingway became passionately involved in deep-sea fishing for marlin and tuna. Like his deep lifelong engagement with bullfighting, Hemingway's deep-sea fishing interest and devotion were instantly established. The unknown depths of the Gulf Stream were especially intriguing to Hemingway, and he became increasingly proficient as a saltwater fisherman. Just as the "great white hunter" Phillip Percival had guided him on safari in Tanganyika, so Hemingway would be a Leatherstocking-like pathfinder to others in search of enormous game fish.

Ernest Hemingway owned two books by James Fenimore Cooper: *The Last of the Mohicans* and *The Two Admirals: A Tale of the Sea.* These two novels provide an intriguing entrance into Hemingway's understanding of the natural world. Nathaniel Philbrick calls Cooper "the originator of the sea novel," and his ability to write convincingly about both the land and the sea earned Hemingway's admiration (xiii). At a time when Hemingway was increasingly aware of his place in literary history, the Gulf Stream provided a background for him to write himself into the foreground of American culture.[1] Cooper, like Twain and Melville, was a writer who self-consciously shaped an American tradition that Hemingway yearned to be a part of, and the protagonist of his short stories, Nick Adams, is a recognizable descendant of Leatherstocking, Huckleberry Finn, and Ishmael.

Hemingway, like Cooper, created an artistic vision of the land and an equally robust vision of the sea. Hemingway's frontier existed simultaneously as an intellectual construction and, to him, a physical fact. He sought open spaces, in Spain, Wyoming, Africa, or the Gulf Stream, far from the civilization of cities, because he firmly believed in the existence of "wild country," and his hunting and fishing renewed him. Thematically, too, the Gulf Stream presented a stage for exploration, as Hemingway grew to intimately know the sea in a way that would reshape his method of writing. Since 1924, Hemingway had stated that his ambition was to write "like Cezanne painted," and at the publication of *The Old Man and the Sea* in 1952, the Gulf Stream was no longer merely a frontier, for Hemingway had decided he wanted his books illustrated by Winslow Homer.

And though he once saw the Gulf Stream as a frontier, after studying it as a self-taught marine biologist, that view, too, evolved, and according to ichthyologist Henry V. Fowler, Hemingway "revised the classification for marlin for the whole North Atlantic" (Baker, *Life* 264).

In the early 1930s, Hemingway abandoned the novel as a form. Perhaps nervous about following up the overwhelming popular and critical success of *A Farewell to Arms*, he wrote *Death in the Afternoon* (1932), a handbook to bullfighting and an extended commentary on Spanish wine, food, landscape, and art. He then assembled a collection of short stories, *Winner Take Nothing* (1933). He wrote monthly articles for *Esquire* and was paid $500 for each one. And he wrote an account of his two-month African safari, *Green Hills of Africa* (1935). In the midst of this broad range of work, the only constant factor in his life was fishing on the Gulf Stream.

Hemingway's introduction to deep-sea fishing came in 1931 aboard Joe Russell's thirty-two-foot launch, the *Anita*. Russell owned the now-famous Key West bar Sloppy Joe's, and on the side he ran illegal liquor to the United States from Havana. In April of the next year, Hemingway left Key West for Havana, expecting to be gone ten days. That plan was instantly abandoned. According to Michael Reynolds,

Days turned into weeks, weeks into months. Wives came and left;
all taking their turns at the heavy rods. . . . Every day but a few they
fished early and hard, keeping a running account: the log of the good
ship *Anita*. . . . For two months, Hemingway's intensity never less-
ened. His fishing partners came and left, but he continued unsated.
Once, with that same intensity, he was married to trout fishing up
in Michigan; then trout fishing gave way to the corrida. Now, with
Death in the Afternoon in galley proofs, that ten-year passion is wan-
ing. These Gulf Stream days, pursuing fish as large as his imagination, are the beginning of a new pursuit which will last him the rest
of his life. (*1930s* 92)

These days fishing and the nights in Havana would plant new creative
seeds in Hemingway's mind. Hemingway fished the Stream through the
end of June, "completely and utterly satisfied on this as sport, living,
spectacle and exercise" (qtd. in Reynolds, *1930s* 92). The Gulf Stream
also provided him with the reality of freedom; escaping his Key West
home, where his wife and two young children noisily awaited his return, he discovered deep-sea fishing at the stage in his life when the
chains of domesticity might have bound him.

In April 1933, Hemingway again chartered Russell's boat, *Anita*, for
two months of marlin fishing. He would keep a log of his daily experience
in a copy of *Warner's Calendar of Medical History*. By the third week of
July, he had spent more than a hundred days on the Gulf Stream, catching upwards of fifty marlin (Baker, *Life* 243). That was the year, too, that
the Cuban leftist revolution against the dictator, Gerardo Machado, was
reaching its peak, and Hemingway left Havana on August 7, the same
day that soldiers opened fire on citizens who were in the streets prema-
turely celebrating Machado's resignation. Hemingway's exposure to the
Gulf Stream and Cuban politics fired his imagination, providing him
with unexpectedly rich raw material for his fiction.

Hemingway's first articulation of his Gulf Stream frontier appears in
1936. In order to entice him to write for his new men's magazine, in 1933
Arnold Gingrich paid $3,000 toward the purchase of Hemingway's boat,
Pilar. In return, Hemingway's first article for the magazine was about
fishing: "Marlin Off the Morro: A Cuban Letter." In the twenty-five articles that Hemingway wrote from 1933 to 1936, the main subject of
each piece was Hemingway's public persona and his leisure activities.

His frontier article entitled "On the Blue Water: A Gulf Stream Letter" was one of his last pieces for the magazine:

> In the first place, the Gulf Stream and the other great ocean currents are the last wild country there is left. Once you are out of sight of land and of other boats you are more alone than you can ever be hunting and the sea is the same as it has been since before men ever went on it in boats. In a season fishing you will see it oily flat as the becalmed galleons saw it while they drifted to the westward; white-capped with a fresh breeze as they saw it running with the trades; and in high, rolling blue hills the tops blowing off them like snow as they were punished by it so that sometimes you will see three great hills of water with your fish jumping from the top of the farthest one and if you tried to make a turn with him without picking your chance, one of those breaking crests would roar down on you with a thousand tons of water and you would hunt no more elephants, Richard, my lad. (228–29)

The first sentence leaps out: "the last wild country there is left." Hemingway, apparently blind to the fishermen who have been working here for hundreds of years, and the ecological damage his presence may incur, sees the Stream as a place to explore, conquer, exploit.

Yet even within that same article, Hemingway recognizes his own complex feelings for the Gulf Stream: it is not just a space to be conquered. A relationship can be established with the Stream that allows one to heighten one's own human experience through intimate contact with nature. Hemingway continues: "But there is great pleasure in being on the sea, in the unknown wild suddenness of a great fish; in his life and death which he lives for you in an hour while your strength is harnessed to his; and there is great satisfaction in conquering this sea it lives in" (234). The key phrase here, of course, is "in his life and death which he lives for you in an hour while your strength is harnessed to his." A timeless, universal struggle takes place here on the Stream, and Hemingway's life is enriched by this recognition. The unification within the "great fish," to feel his immense vitality while trying to destroy that energy, was one of the great satisfactions of fishing. For Hemingway, it is possible to revere the great fish of the Gulf Stream while simultaneously seeking to kill them, to conquer them. As at this point in his life, he recognized no conflict within his own values.

For him, a wilderness was something that was spoiled and destroyed by the encroachment of civilization, as that contact eroded the regenerative power of nature. In "Big Two Hearted River Part I," Nick laments the "burned over country" but finds solace in watching trout in a stream: "They were very satisfactory" (*In Our Time* 134).

Outside of his creative work, Hemingway referred to the natural world around him using a language of frank assessment that jars us today. In an *Esquire* letter entitled "He Who Gets Slap Happy," Hemingway wrote:

> America has always been a country of hunters and fishermen. As many people, probably, came to North America because there was good free hunting and fishing as ever came to make their fortunes. But plenty came who cared nothing about hunting, nothing about fishing, nothing about the woods, nor the prairies . . . nor the big lakes and small lakes, nor the sea coast, nor the sea, nor the mountains in summer and winter . . . nor when the geese fly in the night nor when the ducks come down before the autumn storms . . . nor about the timer that is gone . . . nor about a frozen country road . . . nor about leaves burning in fall, nor about any of these things that we have loved. Nor do they care about anything but the values they bought with them from the towns they lived in to the towns they live in now; nor do they think anyone else cares. They are very sure no one cares to read about hunting and fishing because they don't. So I say to hell with them. (19)

By embracing the beauties of the Gulf Stream and elsewhere, Hemingway was rejecting the narrowness of an urban perspective and declaring emphatically that the beauty of the American landscape was a solitary pleasure that must be experienced to be understood. Eight months later, in "On the Blue Water: A Gulf Stream Letter," Hemingway extended this train of thought:

> Because the Gulf Stream is unexploited country, only the fringe of it ever being fished, and then only at a dozen places in thousands of miles of current, no one knows what fish live in it, or how great size they reach or what age, or even what kinds of fish and animals live in it at different depth. When you are drifting, out of sight of land, fishing

four lines, sixty, eighty, 100 and 150 fathoms down, in water that is
700 fathoms deep, you never know what may take the small tuna that
you use for bait. . . . It may be a marlin that will jump high and clear
off to your right and then go off in a series of leaps, throwing a splash
like a speedboat in a sea as you shout for the boat to turn with him
watching the line melting off the reel before the boat can get around.
Or it may be a broadbill that will show wagging his great broadsword.
Or it may be some fish that you will never see at all that will head
straight out to the north-west like a submerged submarine and never
show and at the end of five hours the angler has a straightened-out
hook. There is always a feeling of excitement when a fish takes hold
when you are drifting deep. (238–39)

The remote, "unexplored" nature of the Stream would at first enthrall
Hemingway and later inspire him to immerse himself in the vocabulary
and practices of marine biology. It is intriguing to note how Hemingway's language establishes his dual perspective; he is unapologetically a
hunter of big fish, but also appreciative of the natural mysteries of the
Gulf Stream.

Hemingway's unintentional advertising in *Esquire* was also an un-
subtle admission of his longing for company. Far away from intellectual
equals and practicing writers, Hemingway launched a steady stream of
letters to friends such as Archibald MacLeish, John Dos Passos, and
Max Perkins to join him on the Gulf Stream. In an April 8, 1933, letter
to Janet Flanner, Hemingway wrote:

Look, why don't you come to Havana? I'm going over there in three
days in a thirty four foot boat fixed up for fishing. We fished along
that coast 65 days last year, from this time on. It is wonderful. The
gulf stream [*sic*] runs almost black and comes right in to the shore.
The marlin swordfish go by, swimming up the stream like cars on
a highway. You go in to shore in the boat and look down to see the
wrinkles in the white sand through the clear water. It looks as though
you would strike bottom. They have beaches miles and miles long,
hard white sand and no houses for twenty miles. We go out in the
morning and troll the stream go in to swim and get back somewhere
at night. Sometimes sleep on the boat. Sometimes on the town. (*Selected Letters* 386–87)

The Gulf Stream was a garden of pleasures and plenty to share with deserving and appreciative guests.

Thus, in the midst of his fragmented life of the 1930s, Hemingway's singular preoccupation was the Gulf Stream. The height of the marlin season runs from late April to August, and from 1932 to 1937, Hemingway arranged his life to spend those months on the Gulf Stream. Fishing logs exist from 1932, 1933, 1934, 1936, and 1939.[2] To read the logs carefully is to recognize that Hemingway's creative life and his broader understanding of the natural world were in constant metamorphosis. One day with stunning aggression he would pursue a pod of whales with a harpoon, and the next he would dwell on the beautiful colors of a marlin's stripes. Hemingway sought to kill the same animal life he revered. Yet to him there was no inconsistency in this behavior. Raised by a physician father who was a serious naturalist, hunter, and fisherman, by the 1930s Hemingway had reconciled the paradox of his pursuit of game with a very serious conservation ethic. These two perspectives that existed as Hemingway's duality would be transformed by his immersion in the Gulf Stream.

The Gulf Stream was very much on Hemingway's mind when he was on his safari in Tanganyika from December 20, 1933, to February 28, 1934. Hunting on the African frontier and fishing the Gulf Stream were parallel activities for Hemingway: both settings placed him in an environment where he could define himself within the context of enduring natural forces. The harsh African landscape contrasted jarringly with the fertility of the Gulf Stream, churning Hemingway's imagination. When he returned to Key West, he immediately resumed his fishing schedule and began composing *Green Hills of Africa*. Not a novel, nor a traditional travel narrative, *Green Hills of Africa* gives further evidence that Hemingway was a writer in metamorphosis throughout the 1930s. In the foreword, Hemingway wrote: "The writer has attempted to write an absolutely true book to see whether the shape of a country and the pattern of a month's action can, if truly presented, compete with a work of imagination" (iii). The phrase "absolutely true" carries extra weight and signals that Hemingway is focusing on observation. Like the minutiae of the fishing logs, the experience of Africa must be given over to the reader through details of meals, weather, conversations, and animals. It would be in *Green Hills of Africa* that Hemingway would make his longest and most lyrical evocation of the Gulf Stream as a unifying symbol for humanity, foreshadowing the

themes of *The Old Man and the Sea*. The passage is central to understanding the Gulf Stream's importance to Hemingway in the years he was
preparing the fishing log. Hemingway begins:

> If you serve time for society, democracy, and the other things quite
> young, and declining any further enlistment make yourself respon-
> sible only to yourself, you exchange the pleasant, comforting stench
> of comrades for something you can never feel in any other way than
> by yourself. (148)

In the first few lines, Hemingway is responding to the critics of *Death
in the Afternoon* and his articles in *Esquire*, affirming that this writing has "value absolutely." Affirming the connection between Africa
and the Gulf Stream through the euphoria of his frontier individualism,
Hemingway expresses his disdain for the fashionable Marxism sweep-
ing across urban intellectual circles. He continues:

> When, on the sea, you are alone with it and know that this Gulf
> Stream you are living with, knowing, learning about, and loving, has
> moved, as it moves, since before man, and that it has gone by the
> shoreline of that long, beautiful, unhappy island since before Colum-
> bus sighted it and that the things you find out about it, and those
> that have always lived in it are permanent and of value because that
> stream will flow, as it has flowed, after Indians, after the Spanish, after
> the British, after the Cubans and all the systems of governments, the
> richness, the poverty, the martyrdom, the sacrifice and the venality
> and the cruelty are all gone as the high-piled scow of garbage, bright
> colored, white-flecked, ill-smelling, now tilted on its side, spills off
> its load into the blue water, turning it a pale green to a depth of four
> or five fathoms as the load spreads across the surface, the sinkable
> part going down and the flotsam of palm fronds, corks, bottles, and
> used electric light globes, seasoned with an occasional condom or
> a deep floating corset, the torn leaves of a student's exercise book,
> a well-inflated dog, the occasional rat, the no-longer-distinguished
> cat; all this well-shepherded by the boats of the garbage pickers who
> pluck their prizes with long poles, as interested, as intelligent, and as
> accurate as historians; they have the viewpoint; the stream with no
> visible flow, takes five loads of this a day when things are going well

in La Habana and in ten miles along the coast it is as clear and blue and unimpressed as it was ever before the tug hauled out the scow; and in the palm fronds of our victories, the worn light bulbs of our discoveries and the empty condoms of our great loves float with no significance against one single, lasting thing—the stream. (148–50)

The Gulf Stream exists outside the structure of human-made time, fashion, and empires, and the power of its current absorbs the real and metaphorical garbage generated by civilization. To Hemingway, art connected to a regenerative muse endures, as the Stream renders other transitory preoccupations of man irrelevant. Inscribing himself within its metaphorical waters, Hemingway thus draws strength for the indifference of his position from the Stream, which "will flow, as it has flowed."

Here Hemingway is also outlining what he considered the symbolic potential of the Gulf Stream. In the preface to the first printing of *Virgin Land: The American West as Symbol and Myth,* Henry Nash Smith stated that "myth" and "symbol" were used to designate "the same kind of thing, namely an intellectual construction that fuses concept and emotion into an image" (xi). Earlier in the passage in *Green Hills of Africa,* Hemingway unites the "feeling" that "comes when you write well and truly of something" to the symbolic reality of the Gulf Stream, something that is "blue" in its purity and God-like in its indifference to the venality of man (148). In his creation of an Eden-like image of the Gulf Stream, Hemingway is outlining the symbolic terrain for *To Have and Have Not* and *The Old Man and the Sea.* They will take place in a seascape imagined both as a timeless, fertile space and as an actual site of human-made violence and predatory fishing. In the scope of his language, Hemingway is revealing that his symbolic Gulf Stream is, at this point, unreconciled with his activities, as there is no recognizable conflict between sport and nature.

Also in *Green Hills of Africa,* Hemingway made his first comments about Herman Melville. Hemingway's discovery of the Gulf Stream coincided with the Melville Revival of the late 1920s.[3] Publication of Raymond Weaver's *Herman Melville, Mariner and Mystic* (1921), Melville's posthumous "Billy Budd, Foretopman" (1924), and Lewis Mumford's *Herman Melville: A Study of His Life and Vision* (1929) sparked a reevaluation of his work by students of literature and history (Robertson-Lorant xv). By 1932, when Hemingway was fully confronting the Gulf Stream for the first time, "the vogue of Herman Melville was at its peak" (Shumway 180). Hemingway wrote:

> We have had writers of rhetoric who had the good fortune to find a lit-tle in a chronicle of another man and from voyaging, of how things, ac-tual things, can be, whales for instance, and this knowledge is wrapped in rhetoric like plums in a pudding. Occasionally it is there, alone, unwrapped in pudding, and it is good. This is Melville. But the people who praise it, praise it for the rhetoric which is not important. They put a mystery in that is not there. (*Green Hills of Africa* 20)

Although Hemingway does not admire the language Melville used to transform his own experiences into fiction, he recognizes a shared ap-preciation for the "plums," or actual observations of the whales. In 1934, Hemingway professes not to believe in the "mystery" of the whales that was so important to Melville. Instead, he approaches the natural world from the viewpoint of a scientist and a hunter.

From his father, Hemingway inherited the intellectual underpinnings to make sense of the Gulf Stream. Although he never went to college, from an early age, Hemingway was educated to be a scientist. In an arti-cle aptly titled "Eye and Heart: Hemingway as Naturalist," Susan Beegel writes:

> At Oberlin, Ed Hemingway became a member of the Agassiz Asso-ciation, an organization honoring the memory of the great Swiss-American scientist Louis Agassiz (1807–1873), founder of Harvard University's Museum of Comparative Zoology, of our National Academy of Science, and of the prototype field station that would be-come the Marine Biological Laboratory at Woods Hole. The Agassiz Association was devoted to amateur nature study through fieldwork out-of-doors, a concept Agassiz pioneered with Swiss schoolchildren and helped to popularize in America. (68)

His father, an obstetrician, would found an Oak Park chapter of the Agassiz Association. According to Beegel, "Ernest's early training in the Agassiz method by his father was reinforced by the Oak Park school system which also emphasized object-oriented science education" (70). Beegel quotes Agassiz: "Train your pupils to be observers, and have them provided with the specimens about which you speak. Teach your children to bring them in themselves, take your text from the brooks, not from the booksellers" (69). The mature Hemingway had absorbed much of the Agassiz method and was creating an intersection of science and art as he sought to "represent the whole" (Beegel 69) in his writing. The metaphorical power of the Stream combined with Hemingway's boyhood education to establish a framework for his observations. Hemingway recognized the scientific importance of the Stream, as well as its potential to regenerate his fiction.

Thus, he was to provide ample record of his enthusiasm for understanding the Gulf Stream. Perhaps the least explored section of the entire Hemingway Collection at the John F. Kennedy Library in Boston is the fishing logs. More than any other documents, they reveal the daily minutiae of Hemingway's life in the 1930s. Dense in observed detail, they give convincing evidence of Hemingway's education as an aspiring marine scientist, while showing his progression from a novice saltwater fisherman to an acknowledged expert who contributed to authoritative texts such as *American Big Game Fishing* (1935), *Atlantic Game Fishing* (1937), and *Game Fish of the World* (1949).

The basic form begins with a notation about the fuel status, the weather (sky, clouds, wind, temperature), a description of the Gulf Stream, a list of passengers, and the time of departure. The fishing logs are written in English, but Hemingway uses Spanish names for the marine life.[4] The Cuban fishermen refer to sharks as *dentuso,* and dolphins as *dorado.* Writing in 1935, Hemingway noted the struggle to identify the different species of marlin: "White marlin are called *aguja blanca,* striped marlin are called *casteros* or *aguja de casta;* black marlin are called *pez grande,* or *aguja negra.* Blue marlin are confounded with the black but are called sometimes *azules* or *aguja bobos*" ("Marlin Off Cuba" 81). This Cuban vocabulary was completely new to Hemingway when he first fished from Joe Russell's *Anita* in 1931. In bullfighting and big game hunting, Hemingway had been an autodidact, creating his own reading lists and asking questions of acknowledged experts. Just as he had learned about modernism at the knee of Gertrude Stein, Hemingway would learn about fishing at the knee of Carlos Gutierrez.

A Cuban commercial fisherman, Gutierrez had been fishing the Gulf Stream since 1884, when he was six years old (Baker, *Life* 228). Since 1912, the fifty-four-year-old Gutierrez had been keeping a record of all his catches, with dates and weights. Hemingway, the good student, would follow his example. Taking place on July 14, 1932, the first conversation between Hemingway and Gutierrez was transcribed by Hemingway himself, and scribbled onto the cover of a Standard School Series marble notebook, his first makeshift log. Writing in fragmented sentences, Hemingway took down Gutierrez's responses to his questions. Since the encounter was so crucial to Hemingway's education, it is quoted in full:

(1) Carlos—Captain of Ferrer
His record 57 small—18 big
fish completely alive—in one season
longest ever 45 arrobas[5]
Cabanas
Black marlin—Bobos
bite at anything
all come to the surface with E wind
—seen 30 in a day—
spawning habits—tail to tail—
female headed into current—
mail [sic] receiving eggs in gills—
has seen this
favorite food of Big Marlin is small tuna or albacore
big fish will take bait in sardines
roe of marlin weighs 41 lbs
hooked one in eye bulbed and
weighed out at 1 lb 2 ounces
(2) April–May small ones then [illegible]
stuffed marlin in June and
July on black marlin August
Sept October until and including Northers
Current runs strong
and very dark between August and September
[illegible]
But year last
has seen as many as 100 small
marlin by then—has all four
lines came taut and looked and
seen marlin below and all around
males always looking for females

pair when find them
male rush boat and refuse
to leave when female hooked
Black marlin swallow bait and hook [illegible]
hook pulls out stomach and kills them quickly
(3) occasionally hook them in
mouth then will go out
400 feet walking on tail
jumping
man who got huge black marlin haves
cut to bone and lost him when stomach pulled out
Carlos had one could not get
into boat and sharks bit off all
except head and [shoulders?]
which weighed 12 arrobas
[illegible] marlin of 24 arrobas
small tuna of 40 lbs from
stomach of one (must ask may have got weight wrong)
Go off into direction of Mexico
when leave all came to the
surface with East wind large
ones run as plentifully as small ones
(4) worst biting winds are SW
N but East
best places on coast are
Boca Varuco and Cabanas
Gulf Stream closest here
figure between shark
and porpoise
giant whale sharks—elefantas—
black and white—plentiful in August
weary at Café San Antonion
(5) Black marlin Carlos hooked
sounded 11 cordeles of 45 fathoms
each 495 fathom straight down
another sounded in 300 fathoms
and broke his sword on the
bottom

> king fish come in May inside the reef—
> wahoo come in November
> December go in March—*Carlos has had an aguja*
> *jump over the boat—hooked four*
> *at once when alone—landed*
> *three*—says black marlin
> may run to a ton in May at
> see some that look like whales

Through examples from the extremes of his own experience, Gutierrez educates Hemingway in the basic parameters of the marlin season, explaining breeding habits and how to hook them. What Hemingway writes down indicates what he did not know and provides the index for his subsequent education. The image of an *aguja* (black marlin) getting so large that it looked like a whale and may leap over a man alone in a small boat surely would have stimulated Hemingway's Melville-fed imagination. Hemingway's transcription of Gutierrez's lecture also set the pattern for his own log entries; if possible, everything about the Gulf Stream should be quantified: the swiftness of the wind, the depth of the water, the gasoline left in the tanks, the barometric pressure, and so forth.

In this initial fishing log entry were also two seeds that would germinate during the composition of *The Old Man and the Sea* (see the language in italics). Hemingway's transcription reads: "Carlos had one could not get—into boat and sharks bit off all—except head and [shoulders?]—which weighed 12 <u>arrobas.</u>" (The twelve-arroba skeleton weighed 300 pounds.) Also notable is the loyalty of the marlin to its mate. Hemingway would revisit this aspect of marlin behavior in his essay "Marlin Off Cuba" and in the novella. Janice Byrne correctly asserts that this interview demonstrates that "Hemingway began gathering material for *The Old Man and the Sea* possibly as early as 1932 and continued to record and refine his data thereafter" (70).[6] Hemingway would see many more apple-cored marlin, and doubtless he drew on a multitude of memories from the fifteen years that transpired before he began composing *The Old Man and the Sea* in 1947. As others have noted, it is impossible to support a single marlin theory.

The log from May contains images that surely stimulated Hemingway's imagination. As Hemingway describes them, the marlin frequently demonstrate humanlike qualities. They begin to act like characters in a children's fable:

May 11
Carlos tired of seeing same
huge black marlin identified by
scar in three successive days
in the deep hole opposite
the Morro—4th day was gone—
Also about marlin 18 arrobas
swamping the boat—also
huge black marlin pulling
the bow under—

Portrayed as a creature of habit, the marlin, already wounded and battle weary, is protecting a home, perhaps containing roe. The image of
the scarred marlin echoes the characterization of the marlin in *The
Old Man and the Sea:* fighting back, steadfast, noble. Throughout the
month, careful attention is paid to the nuances of marlin behavior. On
May 18, he records:

. . . .

at 2pm saw big marlin
behind bait on surface he
rushed it but refused it
each time when slacked or
else took it by the tail only
acted sly as though he had been hooked

In the effective structure of his description—"rushed it but refused
it"—Hemingway captures the action of the fish while also noting its
discriminating intelligence. Marlin can learn, and they toy with humans.
Hemingway attributes cunning intelligence to the marlin in the same
way that Melville does to Moby-Dick. As his fishing season ended,
Hemingway had rich imagery gestating in his mind.[7]

Other passages in the log celebrate the rejuvenating powers of the
Stream, affirming again Hemingway's understanding of it as a pastoral
space. On May 15, Hemingway writes:

. . . .

Pauline had (good) strike-fish
took 50 yards line pulled out

at 1220—as we were going
[illegible] beach above pavilion—
most wonderful water and
swimming ever in my life—
coming out at 230 Grant
hooked marlin (32)[8]

The phrase in italics is striking: "most wonderful water and swimming ever in my life." Hemingway's impression is immediate, unfiltered, and unadorned. This experience was one of the most marvelous of all those in his thirty-two years of life. The waters of the Gulf Stream transformed Hemingway; they were unique, fertile, life giving. At a time in his life when he felt besieged by urban critics, they were a whole new world.

The form of each log entry is similar, but the texture of each day differs. On the seventeenth of May, Hemingway recorded:

EH hooked Marlin opposite
Cojimar 2 jumps threw hook—930
swam at beach 3pm saw
first big striped marlin tail at least
three feet behind teaser deep down
Back a foot or more across
came to surface and when we
curled boat but [illegible] down before
we saw baits (sky was very overcast) and had
strike from another marlin

Hemingway records here the excitement of sighting a marlin with a back "a foot or more across," which means it was a black marlin in excess of five hundred pounds. The narrative approach to the document of the log is notable as well. Hemingway refers to himself in the third person through his own initials, in case someone else needed to review the log. He wants a detailed document that can be offered as evidence to a record keeper in case he needs to verify a catch. He also uses scientific details to record his observations, as he wants the log to be a testament to his experimental fishing. He is trying to create an objective document, not a personal narrative. Important, too, is his insertion of the qualification of the weather conditions when the large marlin appeared: "sky was very overcast." Hemingway is seeking to find a connection between the weather above the water and the behavior of the fish below the surface.

By the time Hemingway resumed marlin fishing in 1933, much had happened in his life. He had hunted from July to October in Wyoming. *Death in the Afternoon* had been published to deeply unsatisfying reviews.[9] And Hemingway had driven from Key West to Piggott, Arkansas, for the holiday season. When the dust had settled, and Hemingway finally found himself back on the deck of the *Anita* on January 25, his passion for fishing had crystallized. It was a narcotic-like alternative to the complicated world on land.

Hemingway planned to take the *Anita* over to Havana for another season of marlin fishing, but he was a little uneasy about the unpredictable nature of Cuban political tensions. In a letter to Max Perkins, Hemingway wrote:

> In case of getting into jam in Cuba (know a few too many people there) I may ask you to give me a paper saying this will certify that Ernest Hemingway is at work on a book dealing with the migratory fish of the Gulf Stream, their habits and capture with special reference to the fishing in Cuban Waters from a sporting standpoint. The book on which Mr. Hemingway is working will be published by Charles Scribners Sons, 597 Fifth Avenue, New York City. Articles will be published on this subject by Scribners Magazine. I wish you would have this made out To Whom It May Concern and typed on your most impressive stationery and signed, say, by Charlie and send it down to me now. In a time of revolution it might keep me from getting shot and it would most certainly help me with the book. . . . Won't get you into any trouble and you needn't publish the book or articles either if you don't wish. But need some sort of strong credentials. (*Only Thing* 184–85)

The reference to a Gulf Stream book is intriguing. Hemingway could simply be providing Perkins with some background for the letter. More interesting, however, is the idea of a book "dealing with the migratory fish" in "Cuban Waters from a sporting standpoint." The conception seems to parallel *Death in the Afternoon,* which, one could argue, deals with bulls in Spain from a "sporting standpoint." The plan, however, seems to be for a book completely unlike *To Have and Have Not,* which he would start in February 1933. The nature, too, of his engagement with Cuban politics is clearly that of an observer, not a participant, and unlike the civil war in Spain, the Cuban revolution was an issue on which he would not, at this point, take a side.[10]

On this trip, Hemingway would also be gathering material for the first issue of *Esquire*, which would appear in the fall of 1933. The breezy articles Hemingway produced stand in deep contrast with the apprehensiveness he expressed to Perkins. The first two paragraphs of "Marlin Off the Morro" capture the spirit of privileged, careless leisure that would permeate all of Hemingway's writing for the magazine. The article begins:

> The rooms on the north-east corner of the Ambos Mundos Hotel in Havana look out, to the north, over the old cathedral, the entrance to the harbour, and the sea, and to the east to Casablanca peninsula, the roofs of all houses in between and the width of the harbour. If you sleep with your feet towards the east . . . the sun, coming up over the Casablanca side and into your open window, will shine on your face and wake you no matter where you were the night before. If you do not choose to get up you can turn around the other way in the bed or roll over. That will not help for long because the sun will be getting stronger and the only thing to do is close the shutter.
>
> Getting up to close the shutter you look across the harbour to the flag on the fortress and see it is straightened out toward you. You look out the north window past the Morro and see that the smooth running sheen is rippling over and you know the trade wind is coming up early. You take a shower, pull on an old pair of khaki pants and a shirt, take the pair of moccasins that are very dry, put the other pair in the window so they will be dry [the] next night, walk to the elevator, ride down, get a paper at the desk, walk across the corner to a café and have breakfast. (139)

Hemingway's narrative persona is a man foreign to Cuba, without a wife and children, relaxed, taking his time, and savoring the pleasures of the Cuban atmosphere as a connoisseur of life. By directly addressing the reader, he draws him enviously into his narrative, presenting him too with the inconsequential choices of a rich, famous man on vacation, untouched by political turmoil.

The log for 1933 has a more evidentiary quality to it.[11] Hemingway was writing down the details of his life in order to keep track of them; he was extremely busy. Yet he was also trying to make a record of events so that he could recover them for his fiction. Thus, for February 7, the log reads: "wrote story—finished it." The story Hemingway is referring to is "One Reader Writes," one of his least imaginative or artistic efforts, in which he transcribes an actual letter from a woman in Harrisburg, Pennsylvania, to Dr. Logan Clendening of Kansas City. Clendening was a friend of Hemingway's and the author of a best-selling book on the prevention of syphilis.[12] The fact that Hemingway would try to count this effort as a short story reveals his discouraged and somewhat strained frame of mind. He had been away from his work too long, and he needed to create something to feel good about.[13]

The next day, February 8, his discouragement seeps through again in the log. Hemingway records: "Pleasant day but bad fishing (almost) worst ever." For Hemingway to call a day the "worst ever" indicates that he is feeling irascible and is still not settled into a new routine after the disorder of the past few months. Hemingway was out of sorts enough to record handing over money to his mate, Bra Saunders, on February 10: "Gave Bra $50 cash." It is impossible to know whether the transaction was a loan or simply payment for work. Yet as a man known for his generosity, his record of the transaction here indicates that the log has taken on an added dimension. It is now an accounting ledger.

As an investigation into how weather affected the fishing, details on the climate are always noted in the logs. The weather was always important and underscores the documentary purpose of the fishing logs; Hemingway's precise observations were deposits to be withdrawn later when he was imagining a setting. Thus, on February 28, Hemingway records:

Nwester
Blew <u>all</u> week
wind went out and blew from SE
on Saturday Sunday Monday Tuesday
March 8 First day able to fish
<u>strong</u> gulf current

By observing the direction of the wind, Hemingway is trying to speculate on its effect on the "<u>strong</u> gulf current," as he hopes to predict a pattern that will lead to better fishing. Hemingway would try to integrate all the natural elements to create his picture of Santiago's experience. As a dimension of the visible world carefully observed and learned from, the wind would have to be in the book.

The density of the details in the log affirm that Hemingway felt almost tied to it. He tried to account for each moment he was on the Stream by thoroughly inscribing through his shorthand the minutiae of the wind, moon, current, and weather. On April 3, the entry reads:

> Bra—George O'Neil—Simon—Pauline, EH
> (In harbor channels) glass 30½ moon
> wind SE went into NW
> very light about 5pm tide ½ ebb
> W Built up in N. Big squall
> wash rain from N at 10pm
> Jack channel full of tarpon
> hook 3 in day light—Pauline
> landed one swell one—Simon lost
> one about 35 lbs—Pauline
> jumped off another
> EH (jack)—George (jack)

Everything he records could influence the quality of the fishing, and Hemingway is accumulating a record that he can sift through later to educate himself on the patterns of the natural world. The range of the elements demonstrates how broadly Hemingway is searching for connections, while his shorthand summary of his own results—"jack"—provides commentary for an otherwise objective, fact-laden account of the day.

Even on days when he did not fish, Hemingway felt compelled to maintain the log, and in many ways, his relationship with it parallels his relationship to a novel he is writing. If he neglects his work for a day, he feels guilty and provides excuses. Thus, on April 16, Hemingway records:

> Easter—Wind light NW
> Didn't fish
> to —— at 1215 for lunch
> stayed afterwards and to suffer [sic]
> drank too much!
> Fishermen saw many small

marlin near shore Saturday—wouldn't bite
refused even live bait

Exclamation points are very rare in Hemingway's writing, but here on this Easter Sunday, Hemingway uses one to celebrate and mourn his hangover. Despite his suffering, Hemingway still was bound to record the most recent fishing information he gathered.[14] A compulsive saver of paper, Hemingway understood that he was creating something that was both a creative resource and a scientific document.

The Morro lighthouse has a recurring presence in all of Hemingway's writing about the Gulf Stream. It represents the safety of the Havana harbor, providing a reference point for all the boats at sea. When Hemingway departed Key West for Cuba on April 12, he recorded the details of his passage and his relief at sighting the lighthouse:

Left Key West 1250PM
Sand Key 140PM
Morro 130AM
good stream about 2 hours out
[illegible]
extraordinary action of porpoises in
front of tankers off sand key
saw glare of Havana 8PM little
current until approaching Cuban coast

Harry Morgan, too, would refer to the Morro when he made the reverse journey, departing Havana for Key West: "I went out the harbor and past the Morro and put her on the course for Key West due north" (*To Have and Have Not* 42). The precise tracking of the passage of time, as well as the Sand Key lighthouse, also would make its way into the novel.

The log for 1933 lacks substantial drama, as Hemingway strives for a scientific precision in his language. The uneventful days of April are dutifully reported in unadorned, workmanlike language. On Tuesday, April 18, Hemingway records:

Fishing uncle Gus, Karl G, Charles, EH
wind light NE
little current
Out at 7:30 wheel struck piece of

> box Carlo overboard to examine wheel
> stayed down over a minute twice
> was piece of wood which floated
> free when engine stopped out of
> harbor by 845

Carlo diving overboard and staying underwater in the busy, polluted Havana harbor is a potentially life-threatening moment, but Hemingway records it in language that denies any crisis or drama, again affirming the log as an objective document. The entry for April 19, when the crew is actually catching fish, is notable for Hemingway's specific descriptions:

> . . . .
> Raised a good small dark marlin
> opposite Belen observatory tower
> followed Charles mackerel bait
> with his fin out but would
> not strike

Hemingway is seeking here a connection between the extended fin of the marlin and the fact that it would not strike. He seems to be hypothesizing that it may have had something to do with the mackerel, or perhaps the behavior is connected to the location. Hemingway is always seeking in the logs to create unity between what is observed and what is unseen.

Again and again in the log there is evidence of the intense responsibility Hemingway felt to maintain a precise document. Hemingway was acutely aware of the passage of time. On April 21 he felt compelled to make entries at 7:45, 8:40, 8:45, 10:15, and 10:25 AM, and 12:45, 1:00, 1:25, and 1:30 PM, finally noting, "in @ 6:00."[15] The long gap between 1:30 and 6:00 PM is explained in an incident that underscores the brotherhood of the Gulf Stream. As the crew of the *Anita* aided another boat, the *Celia*, Hemingway records:

> . . . .
> 1 PM saw two boats together
> and ran over to investigate. <u>Celia</u>
> of Cojimar and another boat with

> small marlin landed and a
> Black Marlin of 26 <u>arrobas</u>
> took pictures gave them
> water and beer

A black marlin of twenty-six arrobas would weigh over six hundred pounds and would be celebrated by the whole community of fishermen (see figure 1). Hemingway would always be quick to use a camera for documentation, and the ritual of the photograph was the culmination of the celebration. Although the sense of brotherhood captured in the log was carried over into *To Have and Have Not,* it is conspicuously absent in Santiago's world. The reader has no idea here whether Hemingway himself enjoyed a moment of camaraderie or if he felt burdened by the obligation he felt to assist the *Celia.* The log is only about what Hemingway observes, not what he feels.

Despite the detached quality of the log, Hemingway would later mine the month of April for images for both *To Have and Have Not* and *The Old Man and the Sea.* Noting each species of marine life he encountered, on April 21 Hemingway writes:

> . . . .
>
> 1015 saw two loggerhead turtles
> hooked up
> 1025 small marlin on surface turning
> in circles in search of bait—circled
> him 6 or 8 times—he turning
> smaller all the time—then went
> down—a few minutes later saw large
> hammer head fin

This image reoccurs in book 3 (Winter) of *To Have and Have Not.* Hemingway crafts a conversation between Harry Morgan and his wife, Marie, prior to their lovemaking. Morgan has already lost his arm in a gunfight. In a passage that is not pleasant to read, Hemingway creates a dialogue with Harry as the first speaker:

> "Listen, do you mind the arm? Don't it make you feel funny?"
> "You're silly. I like it. Any that's you I like. Put it across there. Put it along there. Go on. I like it, true."

"It's like a flipper on a loggerhead."

"You ain't no loggerhead. Do they really do it three days? Coot for three days?"

"Sure. Listen, be quiet. We'll wake the girls." (113)

The loggerhead turtle was listed as a threatened species in 1970, which makes it an apt metaphor for Morgan. Although there is no evidence that Hemingway knew of the decline in the loggerhead population, he certainly must have been aware that they frequently ate the marine debris found floating in harbors. At this point in the novel, Morgan, barely scavenging for a living off the Gulf Stream, has taken on the qualities of a loggerhead, fulfilling Hemingway's deterministic design for the novel. In *The Old Man and the Sea*, Hemingway would again use the image of the loggerheads making love, writing that Santiago "had a friendly contempt for the huge, stupid loggerheads, yellow in their armour-plating, strange in their love-making, and happily eating the Portuguese men-of-war with their eyes shut" (37). Significantly, Hemingway feels liberated here to express his "contempt" for loggerheads in a way that his naturalist design for *To Have and Have Not* restricted him from doing. In the universe of the Gulf Stream, Harry and Marie Morgan are the Darwinian equivalent of scavengers eating the Portuguese men-of-war, "the falsest thing in the Ocean" (35).

One of the more intriguing entries encountered in the 1933 log is the one Hemingway made on Saturday, April 22. The log begins by following the established form, with the time, the weather, the wind direction and speed, and then noting who is on board. Yet the language then evolves into a very deliberately constructed outline of the setting of Santa Cruz, as Hemingway crafts within each line a distinctive image inscribed for later use. Unfortunately, several key words are illegible; as in other entries, Hemingway uses dashes rather than formal punctuation. He wrote:

> . . . .
> saw <u>Celia</u> flying Cuban flag and
> got bill and tail of yesterday's
> black marlin from them—fish
> dressed out 19 <u>arrobas</u>—23 in the[16]
> market—tail measured 49 inches
> across—meat was very dark

and so only sold for 4 cents a
pound. Marlin have sold this
year from 12 to 8 cents a lb.
. . . .
No more strikes as we
trolled to Santa Cruz and went
to look over anchorage or [illegible] wharf
Carlos had not been there
for 30 years at which time
there was a small dock
—No dock now
on left some sort of oil
tanks some sort of factory
nice clear cove—steep
limestone cliffs undercut
by sea—dungy looking
small town—Royal palms
and [illegible] behind [illegible] gauge
RR station labeled Santa Cruz—
car on right bank—saddled
horse—crowd of kids—houses
with balconies overhanging
harbor—Karl's fish was
first marlin we have had a
jump from in 8 days

In the passage, there is nothing that can be directly linked to Hemingway's later fiction. Yet in a log that has been consistently objective, dry, and inquiring, it shows how the purpose of the logs can shift in an instant. The use of poetic language is notable because it reveals how closely aligned Hemingway's scientific inquiry was with his creative impulses. To explore the Gulf Stream scientifically was a creative pursuit, an endeavor that would ultimately yield enhanced, fully informed fiction. From the line "No dock now," the entry has changed; Hemingway is recording specific details that he may want to draw on later for his fiction. He is not recording information that will assist him in fishing; rather, he is isolating the details that will help him reconstruct the scene later. Each phrase, therefore, is like a snapshot, a piece of his experience he is trying to freeze in the log so that, later, sitting in Key

West or Havana, he can revive the place and the moment. A phrase such as "steep limestone cliffs undercut by the sea" is an example of Hemingway's best poetic language, blending his painterly eye with concise representational language, foreshadowing his technique in *The Old Man and the Sea*. The shift in the use of the log also demonstrates again how Hemingway completely integrated fishing the Gulf Stream with his creative life.

Several of the May entries may have been reshaped into the marlin fishing sequence in *To Have and Have Not*. In the novel, Morgan narrates: "I was at the wheel and working the edge of the stream opposite that old cement factory where it makes deep so close to shore and where it makes a sort of eddy where there is always lots of bait. Then I saw a splash like a depth bomb, and the sword and eye, and open lower-jaw and huge purple-black head of a black marlin" (20). In the log entry for May 13, Hemingway wrote:

> . . . .
> Out at 110 trolled to Cojimar
> close to shore—saw one marlin
> opposite *cement factory* and
> a huge *covey of flying fish*—
> made turn and Josie saw
> another marlin with [illegible]
> tail out—too far already
> to catch—opposite target
> range a (black) marlin cut
> across [illegible] from shorewards
> like a dolphin chasing
> fish—bit EH's bait—
> slacked and hooked in second
> slack—at 229 jumped about
> 8 times—gaffed at 234

The location of the two moments is the same. The cement factory would become a regular feature of the log, and a place where Hemingway caught many of his larger marlin. According to Gregorio Fuentes, the first mate aboard the *Pilar*, Hemingway tried to fish the same edge of the Gulf Stream, where the green water met the blue, along a stretch of coastline now called Hemingway's mile. "Hemingway's mile is somewhat longer than the orthodox mile, and was measured from the shooting range in La Cabanas fortress at the mouth of Havana Bay to the House of the Priest (or the Pink House)" (Fuentes 117).[17] Hemingway's entry captures both the thrill of sighting a large marlin and the satisfaction of catching one. Hemingway is particularly interested in the dynamics of the marlin's motion—"like a dolphin chasing fish"—and also what technique was required to hook him. In documenting the number of jumps and the precise time it took to land the marlin, Hemingway is recording for his own satisfaction evidence of his improved skill as a fisherman. The cement factory would be the site of another notable catch on May 17. Again, the language of the log would later appear in *To Have and Have Not*. The log reads:

. . . .

1255 opposite Cojimar and
cement factory big striped marlin
struck EH kingfish bait
in a smash and surge—
slacked him long and hooked
him solid—swung shoreward
and jumped high—came
toward us and jumped again—
out and high toward shore—
fought deep from then on—
came in close to shore—
opposite *cement factory*—
line caught on rock—
broke at 150—line chafed
through along a six inch
stretch nearly through in
two other places—lost about
100 years of line—some evidently
caught on spire of rock when
fish swang [sic] it against
current—EH felt it but [rods?]
but couldn't believe it—seems
impossible to lose a marlin
like that—while broken line
came in we did not know

what had happened—EH fighting
weight of boat swinging in
current which was really like
a mill race—we would
go toward fish—gain line
then [illegible] fish stayed down
and long we throw out
the current would carry
boat away—didn't know
this at the time that it
was strength of fish—
most punishment I ever took—
was a beautiful striped
marlin to weigh 150 lbs
gutted and head off
Carlos said
. . . .

This incident appeared in *To Have and Have Not* more directly than other log entries. Re-creating the moment, Hemingway transformed his own loss of a striped marlin into Mr. Johnson's loss of a blackened marlin. Using the flying fish from the entry of May 13, in the novel Hemingway wrote:

> The nigger was still taking her out and I looked and saw he had seen a patch of flying fish burst out ahead and up the stream a little. Looking back, I could see Havana looking fine in the sun and a ship just coming out of the harbour past the Morro. (13)

When Johnson loses the fish, it is for the same reason that Hemingway did. Morgan explains to him:

> "Listen," I told him. "If you don't give them line when they hook up like that they break it. There isn't any line will hold them. When they want it you've got to give it to them. You have to keep a light drag. The market fisherman can't hold them tight when they do that even with a harpoon line. What we have to do is use the boat to chase them so they don't take it all when they make their run. After they

make their run they'll sound and you can tighten up the drag and get it back." (18)

Although Hemingway, the relative novice, would lose the actual fish in 1933, in the novel, Hemingway uses the voice of Morgan, the expert, to chastise and educate Johnson, the urban outsider and fishing amateur. A few pages later, Hemingway recycles the simile of the mill race:

> About four o'clock when we're coming back close in to shore against the Stream; it going like a mill race, us with the sun at our backs; the biggest black marlin I ever saw in my life hit Johnson's bait. (19)

The mill race is meant to illustrate the motion of the Gulf Stream current; in the middle of the Stream it flows eastward, and along the edges, it flows westward.[18] A fishing boat leaving Havana benefits from the current as it heads out for the day, and again when it returns to harbor. For the thirty-three-year-old Hemingway, this battle with a striped marlin was "the most punishment I ever took," and it is one of the few places in the log in which he used underlining for emphasis.

Evidence of Hemingway's evolving understanding of the Gulf Stream is present throughout the 1933 log. Initially, every lost fish was an occasion for expressions of disappointment and assigning blame, but by May, Hemingway is becoming more of a connoisseur of the battle. On the eighteenth of May, he created a detailed entry:

> . . . .
> opposite rifle range Julie saw
> tail of fine striped marlin
> about 3 feet of tail out of
> water—we chased him—he
> came to right teaser—then
> to left—EH bait teaser away
> from him while reeled in
> marlin struck was hooked—
> jumped to left—ahead of
> boat—chased him—he went
> to NE jumping—got belly
> in line—we chased him—-

> EH working to get belly out—
> jumped 8 times in huge
> bounds—broke line against
> belly on 12th jump—
> beautiful striped marlin
> of about 150 lbs.—4th
> striped marlin we've lost
> today—4th well hooked
> fish lost today

The deliberate repetition of the phrase "we chased him" demonstrates that Hemingway crafted this entry to capture the drama of the moment. Although they lost the fish on the twelfth jump, Hemingway's admiring summation—"beautiful striped marlin"—masks any disappointment. Indeed, without the fish, the long log entry becomes the only evidence Hemingway would have to show for this extraordinary moment, and he takes care to re-create it in precise detail.

The next day, Hemingway again experiences a moment on the Gulf Stream to savor and draw on in his fiction. No longer just a sportsman preying on the fish, Hemingway's perception of the Stream is expanding. He records:

> . . . .
> at 535 hooked marlin opposite
> *cement factory*—Bumby strike[19]
> at same time—fish jumped
> 24 times—rode a tail like
> a flying fish—tail slowing
> threw hook on first jump and
> was re-hooked at the base of
> Dorsal fin—*never saw finer*
> *jumping—mate followed him*
> *to boat*—refused Bumby's
> bait—gaffed at 605 PM
> took photographs—sky
> overcast

The log from 1932 was a dry, objective document, but here, Hemingway is providing commentary and imposing his own evaluation on the natural world, as the twenty-four jumps represent something exceptional to Hemingway; he "never saw finer jumping." More importantly, however, are the lines that follow: "mate followed him to boat—refused Bumby's bait." In *The Old Man and the Sea*, Hemingway would write about the mate of a marlin refusing to leave a hooked female fish: "He was beautiful, the old man remembered, and he had stayed" (50).

> He remembered the time he had hooked one of a pair of marlin. The male fish always let the female fish feed first and the hooked fish, the female, made a wild, panic-stricken, despairing fight that soon exhausted her, and all the time the male had stayed with her, crossing the line and circling with her on the surface. He had stayed so close that the old man was afraid he would cut the line with his tail which was sharp as a scythe and almost of that size and shape. When the old man had gaffed her and clubbed her, holding the rapier bill with its sandpaper edge and clubbing her across the top of her head until her colour turned to a colour almost like the backing of mirrors, and then, with the boy's aid, hoisted her aboard, the male fish had stayed by the side of the boat. Then, while the old man was clearing the lines and preparing the harpoon, the male fish jumped high into the air beside the boat to see where the female was and then went down deep, his lavender wings, that were his pectoral fins, spread wide and all his wide lavender stripes showing. (49–50)

The contrast between the eight words written in the log and the fully developed passage in the novella is sharp, yet the figure of the loyal mate is present in both.[20] Hemingway would draw immediately from the logs for scenes in *To Have and Have Not* and then, later, carefully expand recorded kernels such as this one into heavily weighted passages in *The Old Man and the Sea*. The log shows too that even in a matter of months, in his appreciation of the Gulf Stream Hemingway could shift from seeing it as a space of conquest, as his character Harry Morgan does, to subtly savoring the natural world, a trait that would characterize Santiago.

Just as the reader begins to find a pattern in the content and language of the fishing logs, Hemingway would create something unexpected.[21] The entry of June 3, 1933, demonstrates again how Hemingway began to use the logs as a more intimate literary journal when inspired by his surroundings. The long entry begins in the morning and evolves into an imagist poem that documents Hemingway's day.[22] Although it is long, it is a remarkable example of the shifting purposes of the logs, and since it has not been examined elsewhere, it deserves to be quoted in full:

Cabanas—June 3
Left at 7am on a flat calm cloudy, a mist
rising from bay,—mountains a
pale blue, royal palms black as
p—— [illegible], white huts like the
mist—urn burial—
rising fish and shoal of fish
breaking metallic calm—
long line of mountains
Bay made up of many lagoons
old Spanish blockhouse and
fort on point—
high hill of mahogany and
cedar below bay and sea
[illegible] green of young cove
new church on hill
one street town up from water
Ferreleria Viscayara—Hotel
("Len Ser")—Cuartel of Guradia
Rural—bien customs [illegible]
horses—calves—poultry—women
old fort round storehouse
sexseceded [sic] wooden pavillion tops
slave stables and house behind
stone wall
steep roofed thatched houses
(on left below light house)
like Valencian barraca
light at hill
red roofed house—steel framed
skeleton tower for light
across channel by right
beautiful wooded hills—
tall palms against morning sun—
fisherman in channel

freighter aground [illegible]
Looking back—old fort
line of grey trunked palms
wide tops
rising line of grey blue
mountains
the bay already open on both sides—
hills covered with royal palms
leaning toward the mountains—
red roofed house on Cayo Suacio
to left looks in—outside
long sand beach—
a point where houses under cieba
hills—pale green of cane—
the mountains showing dark
softly notched—to the high
rounded coves of Bealicia Honda
at 4am coffee ground—I
breakfast at 6—tortilla—
deviled ham—guava paste—
[illegible]—3 eggs soft boiled
in a glass—Spanish sausages
—champagne cider—coffee
Harbor—buoy that has dragged
(left hand going in) Blue gulf
almost to buoy—aguya boats—
old fashioned equipment—inside
bay—water brown
To left town entrance to river
through mangroves—winding
carpan rolled—saw alligator
often into lagoon [illegible] swelled
river to sea
thousands of egrets
may regret ham
at house—3 bedrooms—kitchen
arrangement—bathroom—porch—
all open—mosquitos
dores colores of pigeons

the two quail crossed path
shooting at buzzards with 22
buzzards came for aguya
entrails—[illegible] of the
pareja
our reception—rolling in pm—
garfish up river—out
caught jack at dark—
suffer—the mosquitos bad
Next morning—early coffee
grinding—breakfast—beat calm
breeze—the [illegible]—
aguya [illegible] soup
she sick—came in at
115 that lunch—wash after lunch
down to boat—ride before suffer
into other part of bay
cocktail 3 jiggers rum—
1 bottle cider-lime-sugar

Each of Hemingway's lines is meant to be distinctive and to later evoke in him a memory of the time in Cabanas, a small harbor west of Havana. Certain phrases have a laserlike precision to them, such as "tall palms against morning sun" and "hills covered with royal palms / leaning toward the mountains." On one level, Hemingway is trying to capture on paper his view of the harbor from the boat and, in that view, see everything. He notes, too, the buildings—a fort, a church, a red-roofed house, a "steel framed / skeleton tower for light," and "steep roofed thatched houses." He notes the animal life: "thousands of egrets," an alligator, mosquitoes, buzzards, garfish, and *aguya* (black marlin). On another level, he is trying to freeze a precise moment to savor, and he layers on the element of appetite, transcribing even what he has put in his stomach: coffee, tortilla, guava paste, three eggs boiled in a glass, Spanish sausages, champagne cider, and deviled ham. The ham, of course, plays into his rhymed line "thousands of egrets / may regret ham," and that small touch adds to the intimacy of the log entry.

More significantly, this entry represents a nexus where Hemingway's earlier method of wanting to "write like Cezanne painted" intersects with his transformation as a writer. The Gulf Stream in Cabanas demands a different formula of composition. The mist, the fish, and the mountains all "rise" here, and the repetition of the word "rise" mirrors Hemingway's use of repetition in the first paragraph of *A Farewell to Arms*. There the dust is "raised" and "rises" from the movement of the troops, a connection that signals how the war disrupts the natural world. Yet Hemingway uses "rising" in the log entry to unify the scene and evoke a harmony within the natural world, showing how humans can be integrated with their environment. The word "rising" thus adds another dimension to his description. He captures the water, "a mist / rising from bay"; the life within the water, "rising fish and shoal of fish / breaking metallic calm"; and the "rising line of grey blue / mountains." In Cabanas, Hemingway is like Santiago, at one with the Gulf Stream; he views the scene from the *Anita*, suspended above the calm water, in the thick of the mist. Indeed, the scene seems to resemble Winslow Homer's 1885 watercolor *Sponge Fishing, Nassau*. In a composition of parallel horizontal elements, Homer shows a view of a wharf from the water, creating a hazy horizon line of palm trees and buildings. There are no mountains. In the words of Helen Cooper, "Against a blue sky almost completely obscured by the pale gray and white clouds, watery strokes of gray and green form the palm trees, while the blinding white light of a Caribbean morning reflecting off the glittering sea is achieved through reserved paper" (135). Quite clearly, Hemingway's poetic log entry foreshadows the style and perspective he would employ fourteen years later, when he began *The Old Man and the Sea*.

CHAPTER 2

The Sea Change Part II

The *Pilar* Log, the International Game Fish Association, and Marlin Theories

HEMINGWAY'S NEXT fishing log—dated July 28, 1934, through February 2, 1935—differs in both circumstance and content from the logs created while he fished from the *Anita*. The intensity of Hemingway's activities seems to hint at turmoil and dissatisfaction within. In the words of Carlos Baker, "In the past year he had fished waters as far apart as the Caribbean Sea and the Indian Ocean. He had witnessed the start of a major Cuban revolution. He had crossed the Atlantic twice and gone from one end of the Mediterranean to the other. He had watched a season of bullfights in Spain, shot pheasant and deer in the Sologne and made a memorable safari in Kenya and Tanganyika" (*Life* 263). In May, his new fishing boat, *Pilar*, arrived in Key West, and Hemingway began writing *Green Hills of Africa*.[1]

When Hemingway returned from Africa, he found waiting for him a letter from Charles B. Cadwalader, director of the Academy of Natural History in Philadelphia. Cadwalader inquired if he would be interested in cooperating with Academy scientists in conducting research in Cuban waters. There was a need to remedy the "lack of knowledge concerning the classification, life histories, food (and) migrations of the . . . sailfish, marlin, tuna and other large game fishes (and) to secure specimens and information in order that our knowledge of these fish may be advanced" (qtd. in Martin 5). Criticism of the number of days that Hemingway spent on the Gulf Stream may have spurred him to promptly invite Cadwalader to join him on the Stream. With *Esquire* providing an audience, Cadwalader's presence would encourage Hemingway to take his observations more seriously in a way that expanded on his boyhood instincts as a naturalist. In his reply to Cadwalader, Hemingway wrote: "It would be very interesting to have a complete collection of these fish and determine scientifically which are truly different species and which are merely sexual and age variations of the same fish" (Reynolds, *1930s* 171). On July 18, when Hemingway and crew arrived in Havana for the marlin season, Cadwalader and ichthyologist Henry Fowler were there to meet him.

Dated July 28, 1934, through February 2, 1935, the log for the 1934 fishing season is also notable for another reason: it is not in Hemingway's hand. Arnold Samuelson, an aspiring writer from Minnesota, had hitchhiked to Key West to question Hemingway about writing and in response was hired as a general helper on the *Pilar*.[2] Despite knowing next to nothing about either fishing or seamanship, Samuelson gamely tried to be of assistance to Hemingway and the rest of the crew. Samuelson's memoir of his experience, entitled *With Hemingway: A Year in Key West and Cuba*, provides a more rounded portrait of life aboard the *Pilar* in the company of professional marine scientists. Indeed, with Fowler and Cadwalader aboard, the fishing log becomes a more exploratory and inquisitive document.[3] Hemingway is trying to add another layer of precision to the log so that he can use it to support his theories on marlin migration and development. According to Linda Patterson Miller, the "log differs significantly from the others in being less provisional and more expansive and detailed. . . . [It] assumes an intricate and sustained narrative weave complete with plot, characters, a protagonist [Hemingway], atmospheric coloring, and emotional heightening" (106).

Most of the entries in the *Anita* logs followed a specific shorthand form, beginning with the time of departure, the temperature, the wind direction, and a list of passengers. The increase in the amount of detail in the 1934 log is striking. The complete entry in the *Pilar* log for July 31 illustrates the change:

July 31
Put in 10 gals gas in port tank (8 inches)
Barometer 30.02. Out at 8.20.
Current far out, school of cero mackerel
jumping in the harbor entrance—
On board, Cadw. Fowler, E.H., A.S., Juan.
Light breeze coming up from the East.

Last night starboard six inches
fifty gal 3½ port 100 gal (o)
fifty gal six-added ten made eight
or forty gal. In market six striped
marlin from 125 to 175 lbs
At ten o'clock off Cojimar raised
a big marlin (250–300) which
came behind EH's bait—then
Cadwalader's, then swerved between
birded back and forth and once
bit EH bait but dropped it.
We made a turn onto a sunny tack and he hit
EH bait but Carlos speed up [sic]
when asked to slow and he
pulled the bait down. Lousy boat
handling—with Josie would have had
the fish by now—saw a Cojimar
fisherman landing what looked
like a marlin coming over found
two mako—took pictures and
Fowler sketched and identified fish
and we took some teeth as
specimens. Was the same kind we
had helped out with a big marlin
two years ago ½ Went in for lunch
and swim at the Punta del
Cobre long beach at 12-30. Out
at 1-45. At 2-25 Juan and
Arnold shouted out that there was
a marlin behind the teaser
(green tease) EH took rod and Juan
was holding with J getting
teaser in got fish to take bait.
Shouted to Carlos to cut out
the engine (we were running
on the little engine). He pulled
down on the lever of the big
engine, result fish feeling pull
at line and leader, jumped and

threw the bait ten feet. Was
a handsome brightly striped
marlin of 125–140 pounds.
At a quarter past four Arnold caught
a 15 pound barracuda on the
feather. Fish had hit so hard on
a tight line that he was hooked in
the gills. We noticed sepia black
oozing from the wound the gaff
made. Carlos opened him and
in the belly found a small
octopus freshly swallowed and
a very large squid that had
been sliced in two pieces.
An hour later at 5:15, Juan
caught a very small barracuda
that would not weigh more than
a pound on the feather. Both
barracuda were in the Gulf
at least two miles from the
edge of the stream. It might be
that the barracuda we catch
far out in the Gulf Stream
in the late spring are there
feeding on the squid.

The density of detail establishes that Hemingway was no longer just creating notes for himself; the document has a full narrative structure, complete characters, and a plot full of digressions. The details are more explanatory than evidentiary. Hemingway notes the bait—"green teaser"—which engine they are using, and the specific mistakes that Carlos makes in boat handling. Hemingway is creating a document that is meant to teach the reader why things happened rather than merely record their occurrence. Now that Fowler and Cadwalader are on board, the fishing trip has become a scientific expedition, and he must create a record of appropriate depth, specificity, and gravity. The log is also meant to supplement the scientific data that they are gathering. Hemingway notes their actions—sketching, taking photos and specimens—and uses his own descriptive language to fill in the scene: "We noticed sepia black oozing from the wound the gaff made. Carlos opened him and in the belly found a small octopus freshly swallowed and a very large squid that had been sliced in two pieces." Hemingway is asking the question, "Why is this barracuda bleeding black?" As a scientist, he must cut it open to find the octopus and the answer to his question. At the same time, he is crafting evocative phrases—"sepia black oozing from the wound" and the "small octopus freshly swallowed"—he is learning about life below the surface of the Gulf Stream.

This fluctuation in the tone and content of the log continues, as incidents that have little to do with the expedition on the Gulf Stream are also recorded in a way that fleshes out the narrative of the summer. On August 5, Hemingway writes:

. . . .
Out at 9.50 after going to
market. Fowler found two new
parrot fish—Mass at San Franciscan church
[illegible] Very little current. Bought
a kingfish off the Morro to have
for lunch and immediately afterward
Arnold caught one on the feather bait.

Although Fowler's discovery of new parrot fish at the market is noteworthy, Hemingway's attendance at Mass is an inclusion inessential to the log, which transforms it again into a diary.[4] And the ironic catch of the kingfish so soon after one was purchased seems to be included only to add color to the narrative.

Hemingway invested more creative energy in these entries as he layered over events to enhance the narrative. On August 8, he relates the details of another fisherman's inability to land a marlin, recording:

. . . .
Went into cove for lunch, swam,
played records, came out at 2:20. At
2:25 off cove EH hooked and
landed a small sailfish which was
under great disadvantage with
too heavy tackle. Hooked on a
mackerel bait and a 140 hook.

Brought in five minutes. He
lunged 8 times but never cleared
the water. No. 3 sailfish 7 feet
5 inches, male, bill about ten
inches long, by weight thirty pounds.
(Log by Arnold)
As we were coming into the
Morro we saw Woodward in a small
boat running in small circles
like a merry-go-round. He said he
had a huge marlin. The merry-go-round
continued with no one making any
effort to fight the fish. . . .

Now that Hemingway has Samuelson's assistance, he has time to create more expansive entries, and the incompetence of the Woodward party seems to be an inconsequential event to record in the log. Yet an image of a merry-go-round, like the mill race in the *Anita* log, would surprisingly reappear in *For Whom the Bell Tolls* (1940):

No, it is not that kind of merry-go-round; although the people are waiting, like the men in caps and the women in knitted sweaters, their heads bare in the gaslight and their hair shining, who stand in front of the wheel of fortune as it spins. Yes, those are the people. But this is another wheel. This is like a wheel that goes up and around.

It has been around twice now. It is a vast wheel, set at an angle, and each time it goes around and then is back to where it starts. One side is higher than the other and the sweep it makes lifts you back and down to where you started. There are no prizes either, he thought, and no one would choose to ride this wheel. You ride it each time and make the turn with no intention ever to have mounted. There is only one turn; one large, elliptical, rising and falling turn and you are back where you have started. We are back now, he thought, and nothing is settled. (225)

The connection here between the images is at first thin. *For Whom the Bell Tolls* is a novel about the Spanish civil war, and in content it has little in common with the events of the summer of 1934. On the Gulf Stream, the merry-go-round parallels the action of characters; in the log,

Woodward always ends up back where he started, unable to catch the fish. In the novel, Jordan is back again where he started, due to the regression in his relationship with Pablo, the leader of the Loyalist rebels.

Yet in theme, the two documents are indeed connected, as both the log and the novel attest to the interconnections between humans and the natural world. From the John Donne epigraph ("No man is an *Illand*, intire of it selfe; every man is a peece of the *Continent*, a part of the *maine*"), Hemingway's novel begins with Jordan lying flat on the "brown, pine needled floor of the forest" and ends as Jordan "could feel his heart beating against the pine needle floor of the forest" (1, 471).[5] The log, too, is about the interconnections between humans and the natural world, as each entry is an inquiry into dimensions of that relationship. In 1940, Hemingway explores this theme through Jordan's relationships with other characters, and his heightened awareness of the natural world. In *The Old Man and the Sea*, the exploration would be continued. Even in 1934, the ideas that would come to fruition in that novella were growing from Hemingway's experiences on the Gulf Stream.

In the August 8 entry, it is noted when Arnold Samuelson wrote in the log. Samuelson's memoir is organized chronologically, so it provides a companion text to the log, expanding further on the characterizations and descriptions. The Friends of the Hemingway Collection bought the carbon copy of the log from the Samuelson estate, and it seems clear that Samuelson used the log as Hemingway would: to ignite his memory and resuscitate details as he composed his memoir. Fashioning a scene that explains his role in the creation of the log, Samuelson wrote:

> I handed E.H. my rod with the feather that was fished between and far behind the two mackerel baits and he held a rod in each hand while I went for the heavy notebook with the silver pencil marking the place. I spent a few minutes every day taking his dictations in the log. It was the one thing I could do better than anybody else on board, Carlos and Juan not being able to write English. I got the logbook and pencil and sat down between E.H. and Cadwalader. "Where did we leave off yesterday?" E.H. asked. "Went into cove for lunch," I said, reading the last sentence in the log. "'Swam, talked to Rutherfords who had lost another teaser on a marlin,'" E.H. dictated, "'trolled back without seeing anything or having any strikes except one small barracuda Maestro caught on a feather coming into the Morro.' Now today. 'On

board Cadwalader, Fowler, E.H., A.S., Carlos Juan. Four blue marlin in the market today, 11, 12, 12, 14 arrobas. Of these three were females and one a male. Out at 9.20. Wind east, freshening, current in close to shore, beautiful dark Gulf water within a quarter of a mile.'" (141)

Samuelson's memoir is especially helpful in creating more complete characterizations of Cadwalader and Fowler, as Hemingway never wrote about their personalities. Introducing them, Samuelson wrote:

We were waiting for the *scientificos*. Marlin had never been classified scientifically, and E.H. was disgusted with the reports of fishermen who were constantly discovering and naming new species. E.H. did not believe the so-called white marlin, striped marlin, silver marlin, blue marlin, black marlin and the giant Tahitian black marlin were different species. He believed they were growth stages and sex and color variations of the same fish. The colors had never been scientifically described because the ichthyologists had only studied them after they were killed and brought in on the dock, by which time their colors had disappeared. In a letter to C.M.B. Cadwalader, Director of the Philadelphia Academy of Natural History, E.H. suggested he send an ichthyologist to Havana to study marlin from the *Pilar* and see the colors of the fish alive in the water. He wanted them scientifically described so that fishermen could identify their catches and know what they were talking about. Cadwalader agreed to send his man down and offered to come himself and pay half the gas. E.H. told him he did not take paying guests but he was welcome to come and fish for ten days, and suggested the gasoline money be used to keep the ichthyologist in Havana for a month so he would be sure to see a variety of fish. E.H. told him to come by the end of July, probably the time of the biggest run this year. (123)[6]

Not masking his feelings, Samuelson described Cadwalader:

Short-legged, slightly pot-bellied, [Cadwalader] always wore the same club-room conversationalist expression on his freckled face, and when he talked to one person he spoke as if he were making a speech to a crowd or speaking for the benefit of those who might be trying to overhear, like a lecturer answering questions of people in his audience. . . .

I had not yet been told that this bachelor philanthropist was the last of a distinguished line of money-making, money hoarding Cadwaladers. It was not until later that I was told he kept twenty-seven servants in his house and was very much upset because an old woman intended to retire and it would be like losing one of the parts in a smooth-running machine. This was the first man I had run into who had so many ancestors and so much money, and I had difficulty understanding him. He would not drink vermouth with us before dinner or wine with his meals or whiskey in the evenings, but would only drink bottled mineral water, and half the mornings he forgot to bring his mineral water and E.H. would have to send Juan ashore for it before we could leave. Cadwalader never gave Juan any money. He must be worried about his investments, I thought. He had to spend so many thousands to keep the museum going and as an economy measure he let E.H. pay for his mineral water. (125)

Clearly, the Midwest-born and -bred Samuelson was unimpressed by the gentleman scientist from Philadelphia.

While Cadwalader and Fowler were aboard, Hemingway would haul in one of the largest marlin of the 1934 season. Samuelson's description of the fish is written under the influence of Hemingway's newly scientific style:

He slammed down hard on the cockpit deck, lying on his side, a huge blue monster, round as a barrel, reaching the full length of the cockpit with his sword in the cabin door and tail almost touching the fish box. . . . The colors divided by a well-defined straight line running from his mouth down the middle of his body to his tail, dark blue above and silver below began fading the instant he came on board, the vivid blue turning almost black and the silver belly darkening to the color of lead. Carlos knelt by the fish's head and kissed it with a loud smack. . . . Henry Fowler drew a sketch of the marlin and E.H. helped him take at least twenty measurements with a steel tape. The fish was twelve feet two inches long from the head of his bill to the tip of his tail, and his girth was four feet eight inches. . . . He tipped [the scale] at 420 pounds, and, tying a rope around his tail, raised him with block and tackle and left him swinging heavily from the scaffold, head down. E.H. sent for Dick Armstrong, the Hearst correspondent; when Dick came, he set the Graflex [camera] on a barrel and, telling everybody to be steady and chasing the kids away, began taking pictures. E.H., holding the fishing rod, stood next to the fish, his guests and crew forming a semicircle around him, and the natives crowded in from all sides in order to be in the picture. (129–30)

Following the established ritual of deep documentation, many photos were taken (see figure 2). Hemingway beams at the camera in the foreground as Cadwalader, small in stature, stands in the background striking a formal pose with his pipe tucked in his mouth. Hemingway sent Samuelson ashore for an extra quart of whiskey, and it became a "night of celebration" (130).

Samuelson's memoir contains important encounters that were not included in the fishing log, two of which may have contributed to elements of *The Old Man and the Sea*.[7] In the first, Samuelson writes:

We traveled three or four miles across the lake to the small town of Cabanas at the foot of the mountain and tied to the low pier, where the barefooted men and naked children had gathered to see the boat. Going ashore, we took a path up a hill past huts built of palm branches, with open doors and windows and no furniture of any kind to be seen inside. We stopped at the top of the hill at an old concrete house with bars across the windows where the town delegate lived and E.H. presented him with the boat's papers. The delegate's son, a market fisherman, gave E.H. the sword of an 800-pound marlin that had towed his skiff three miles out to sea before he could kill it. (117)

The tale contains two key elements of Hemingway's later novella: the towing of a fisherman far to sea and the death of an enormous marlin. Regarding the second, Samuelson states:

The only fishermen who cared to be out in that sea were the young daredevil Chicuelo, who had won the marathon rowing championship by rowing seventy six hours without stopping, and his brother. They were leading all the market fishermen, having brought seven marlin, three well over two hundred and fifty pounds, into the Havana market, while their father, fishing in another boat, had drifted forty five days without a strike. (138)

This episode has another two elements: the figure of the father who has continued to fish despite his prolonged drought, and the contrast between this figure of aged perseverance and youthful vitality as his sons become local success stories in the midst of his defeat. Neither of Samuelson's two tales is recorded in the log, and there is no way to know if they were as notable to Hemingway as they were to him. For Samuelson, however, these two episodes must have reverberated with the published novella.

The lackluster fishing season allowed Hemingway to plunge into the work that would become *Green Hills of Africa,* merging his memory of the landscape of Africa with the reality of the Gulf Stream. Linda Patterson Miller is very astute in assessing the importance of the fishing log as a document that prefigures the book. She writes:

> Hemingway's 1934 *Pilar* log is about seeing "exactly," both in fishing and in art, and it illuminates Hemingway's creative process at a point of personal and artistic change. . . . In 1934 he came back from Africa to follow the Gulf Stream's currents and the marlin's run, whose mystery and unpredictability intrigued him. As he carried in his mind both Africa and Cuba, and went with the current's flow during the 1934 summer, he began to shape a book, *Green Hills of Africa,* that has structural and thematic parallels to his 1934 log. Both these manuscripts, arrived at simultaneously, recreate the thrill and disappointment of pursuit; and they both confirm that memory, rendered timeless through art, is the greatest trophy. (119)

The research that was done from the *Pilar* in August of 1934 was only one form of Hemingway's collaboration with the Academy of Natural Sciences. In later months, Hemingway would send iced specimens from Havana to Philadelphia for Fowler's inspection. Lawrence Martin notes that through 1935, Fowler would make requests of Hemingway, "virtually ordering" him to gather specific marine life. In a letter dated April 22, 1935, Fowler wrote: "We would like you to . . . get samples of . . . the high finned marlin. . . . We would like a small striped marlin. . . . Of the tuna I would like to get a young specimen. . . . [We] would like a specimen skinned out of a large [wahoo] . . . with the first gill arch cut off. . . . I am only concerned with getting the young of" the African pompano (Martin 11). Yet it is also clear that Hemingway was much more than a research assistant to the Academy scientists.

Hemingway's marlin theories were rigorous enough to earn Fowler's respect. In other correspondence, the evidence clearly shows that Fowler built off Hemingway's insights. In a letter from August 8, 1935, Fowler wrote:

> The chances are you are right about the degenerated black marlin. I do not look for any undescribed species. We have certainly too many nominal ones now, and what I am trying to do is to hook up the west Atlantic ones with those of the east Atlantic, or the Madeiras, Canaries, Gulf of Guinea, etc. Over ten years ago I find from galley sheets just going through the press that I had suspected all these marlins to be one and the same species. So far I have nothing to militate against this. Your letter, especially where you speak of variation, seems further vindication. I refer to the asymmetry of the pectoral fins. If at any time you notice further asymmetry in the specimens, that is the fins larger on one side than the other, or apparently rights and lefts, I wish you would bear it in mind and keep details if possible.

This same letter also engages Hemingway on the topic of bluefin tuna, which Hemingway was then fishing in the Gulf Stream in Bimini. Although Hemingway never wrote about tuna in his fiction, again, he had theories about them. Fowler's remarks to Hemingway once more affirm that he respected his opinion on this subject. Fowler wrote:

> The photograph of the small tuna you caught last year and sent to us must . . . be placed with the young of the Great Tuna. Since then I have examined quite a number of our east coast tunas and find that the pale white or grey lines, so clearly shown and contrasted in your photograph, appear that way in the very small specimens. As they grow older a parallel row of spots appear in the alternating inner spaces. This is quite interesting and I would be glad if you kept it in mind with respect to any other albacore or tunas you may happen upon.

In a letter from Cadwalader to Hemingway dated April 16, 1935, it is clear that the Academy was interested in expanding its study into the waters off Bimini, as Cadwalader wrote: "Let me know as soon as you get back from Bimini. By that time I will have more definite information in regard to Fowler's plans and also as to what we could do in cooperation with you in getting some of these fishes studied."

Apparently the Academy of Natural Sciences of Philadelphia was unable to organize a formal study of the bluefin tuna (*Thunnus thynnus*). In the fishing files of the Hemingway Collection, there are four reports from a joint study conducted in 1952 by the University of Miami Marine Laboratory, the U.S. Fish and Wildlife Service, and the Woods Hole Oceanographic Institute. Luis Rene Rivas of the University of Miami supervised the study. The extent of Hemingway's involvement in this study is unknown and requires further research. Hemingway retained the four dense, highly specialized reports alongside his personal newspaper clippings related to fishing. In a letter dated January 20, 1961, less than six months before he committed suicide, Hemingway wrote to Peter Barrett, an author of fishing books: "We're waiting for the weather to clear to go down the coast to the westward again to scout for that Atlantic Bluefin Tuna investigations outfit. Louis Rivas from the Miami University [*sic*] outfit was here yesterday. They are doing a good sound job" (Trogdon 322).

Hemingway's efforts on behalf of the Academy of Natural Sciences were not unappreciated, as Cadwalader later wrote that "with Hemingway's excellent knowledge of these fishes and their habitats, [Fowler] was able to secure enough information in order that they may revise the classification of the marlin insofar as the Atlantic Ocean goes" (Martin 11). For his efforts, Fowler named a species of fish after Hemingway, the *Neorithe hemingwayi*, stating it was for "Ernest Hemingway, author and angler of great game fishes, in appreciation for his assistance in my work on Gulf Stream fishes" ("New Scorpaenoid" 43; see figure 3).

Hemingway's first published theories on marlin migration and breeding appeared in *Esquire* in the fall of 1933. He was free to choose the topic and the length of the article, which took the form of personal essays, labeled "letters." In the premier issue of the magazine, Hemingway wrote:

The white marlin run first in April and May, then come the immature striped marlin with brilliant stripes which fade after the fish dies. These are most plentiful in May and run into June then come the black and striped marlin together. The biggest run of striped marlin is in July and as they get scarce the very big black marlin come through until into September and later. Just before the striped marlin are due to run the smaller marlin drop off altogether and it seems, except for an occasional school of small tuna and bonito, as though the Gulf Stream were empty. There are so many colour variations, some of them caused by feeding, others by age, others by the depth of water, in these marlin that anyone seeking notoriety for himself by naming new species would have a field day along the north Cuba coast. For me they are all colour and sexual variation of the same fish. This is too complicated to go into in a letter. ("Marlin Off the Morro" 140)

Hemingway's speculation that the striped, blue, and black marlin are all variations of the same fish continues, as he writes: "I believe [black marlin] are mostly old, female fish, past their prime and that is age that gives them that black colour. When they are younger they are much bluer and the meat too, is white" (143). It is revealing that Hemingway would so boldly announce his theories when he had only at this time spent two seasons fishing marlin.

Published in August 1934, at the same time that Cadwalader and Fowler were with him, Hemingway's next *Esquire* letter about fishing the Gulf Stream sets forth a series of scientific questions that beg to be answered and expands on his complex, detailed theory of marlin. In "Out in the Stream: A Cuban Letter," Hemingway writes:

Are not the white marlin, the striped marlin and the black marlin all sexual and age variations of the same fish? For me, with what data I have been able to get so far, they are all one fish. This may be wrong and I would be glad to have anyone disprove the theory as what we want is knowledge, not the pride of proving something to be true. So far I believe that the white marlin, the common marlin caught off Miami and Palm Beach, whose top limit in weight is from 125 to 150 lb., are the young fish of both sexes. These fish when caught have either a very faint stripe which shows in the water but disappears when the fish is taken from the sea or no stripe at all. The smallest I have ever seen weighed twenty-three pounds. At a certain weight, around seventy pounds and over, the male fish begin to have very pronounced and fairly wide stripes which show brightly in the water but fade when the fish dies and disappear an hour or so after death. These fish are invariably well rounded, obviously maturing marlin, are always males and are splendid leapers and fighters in the style of the striped marlin. I believe they are the adolescent males of the marlin. (175–76)

Hemingway is eager to unify the gender of the fish in a way that perhaps foreshadows the gender shifts that would occur in the posthumously published novel *The Garden of Eden* (1986). Indeed, Hemingway had titled his 1931 short story of bisexuality "The Sea Change." Hemingway continues:

> The striped marlin is characterized by his small head, heavily rounded body, rapier-like spear, and by the broad lavender stripes that, starting immediately behind the gills, encircle his body at irregular intervals all the way back to his tail. These stripes do not fade much after the fish is dead and will come up brightly hours after the fish has been caught if water is thrown over him. (176)

Hemingway would contrast his acquired, reasoned knowledge against the folk knowledge of the market fisherman, who, untrained in the Agassiz method, had a body of folk knowledge that was not grounded in observation. Hemingway continues:

> Market fishermen say that all the striped marlin are males. On the other hand they claim all the black marlin are females. But what is the intermediate stage in the development of the female of the white marlin from the handsome, gleaming well-proportioned though rather large-headed fish that it is as we know it at 100 pounds, before it becomes the huge, ugly headed, thick-billed, bulky, dark purple, coarse-fleshed, comparatively ugly fish that has been called the black marlin. I believe that its mature life is passed as what we call the silver marlin. This is a handsome, silvery marlin, unstriped, reaching 1,000 pounds or more in weight and a terrific leaper and fighter. The market fishermen claim these fish are always females. That leaves one type of marlin unaccounted for; the so called blue marlin. I do not know whether these are a colour variation stemming from the white, whether they are both male and female, or whether they are a separate species. . . . This time last year we caught a striped marlin with roe in it. . . . But it was roe and the first one any of the commercial fisherman had ever seen in a striped marlin. Until we saw this roe . . . all striped marlin were supposed to be males. . . . Was this striped marlin how shall we put it or as I had believed for a long time, do all marlin white, striped, silver, etc., end their lives as black marlin, becoming females in the process?[8] (176–78)

Frequently addressing the reader directly, Hemingway's casual tone contradicts the earnestness with which he puts forth his theory. In a magazine that served as a showcase for conspicuous consumption in the midst of the Depression, Hemingway, while establishing his credentials as an authority on the subject, is giving his readers perhaps more information than they need.

Hemingway was eager to gain an audience for his theories of how marlin evolve. In his twenty-six-page contribution to Eugene Connett's *American Big Game Fishing*, published in 1935, Hemingway presented his theories once more.[9] In "Marlin Off Cuba," he writes:

> Another possible theory on the blue marlin is that they are from the spawn of the degenerated old black fish, while the striped and silver marlin are bred from fish in their prime. But this is all conjecture and is only put in to start more sportsmen wondering where their fish come from and how and where they go. We know very little about them yet; the sea is one of the last places for a man to explore; and there is wonderful exploring yet for any fisherman who will travel and live for months on the ocean current in a small boat. (78)

"Marlin Off Cuba" is perhaps Hemingway's most exhaustive contribution to marine science and sportfishing in the Gulf Stream. The article contains two maps, both "drawn by Lynn Bogue Hunt from information supplied by Ernest Hemingway." The first map, entitled "Marlin Off Cuba," labels the locations Hemingway can verify as worthwhile to fish. The evaluations range from "very good both well out and in close depending on current" for the area west of Havana to "said to be fair—have not worked it enough to know" for the coastline east of Bahia Honda. According to Hemingway,

> Fishing is good either way from Havana Harbor, to the eastward as far as Jaruco; to the westward as far as Bahia Honda. Fish the edge of the current. If it is out, go out; if it is in close, you can fish right into the hundred fathom curve. A few barracuda will bother you, but there are not many. The biggest marlin are as liable to be close into the edge of soundings as to be far out. Often the current will be well out in the morning and in close in the afternoon. You will find plenty of sharks around the garbage that is dumped out in the current from lighters, but the marlin avoid the discolored water. Stay clear of it or

you can foul a propeller badly. There are good beaches to swim about
twelve miles to the eastward; you can anchor off and swim into the
beach. Don't swim in the Gulf Stream. Sharks really hit you off the
north coast of Cuba no matter what you hear. There is very little feed
and few small fish in the stream; that is probably why the marlin
come there to spawn; and the sharks are very hungry. (80)

The other map is entitled "World Distribution of the Marlins" and has
darkened areas along the coastlines known for good fishing. Hemingway also included seventeen photographs. Twelve of the photos illustrate how to prepare "mackerel bait for trolling for marlin" and were apparently taken by Hemingway. The specificity of the directions below
the photos is a model of economy:

> Hook is drawn out until only eye is left in bait. Then hook is turned
> and point is re-inserted into bait and pushed through to other side. A
> slit is cut along line of the shank so that shank of hook lies parallel
> with backbone and eye of hook is well drawn inside mackerel's gul-
> let. (71)

Four other photos are of trophy marlin, two of which were caught by
H. L. Woodward, a friend of Hemingway's and an American resident
of Havana. The other two photos are of marlin caught by Hemingway,
the 420-pound marlin caught with Cadwalader onboard, and the other
a 343-pound striped marlin. Clearly, Hemingway chose these photos as
advertisements for the Cuban waters, and examples of fish that readers
of Connett's book may catch. Hemingway also includes a photo of a
striped marlin "showing shape of head, fins and stripes" (75). The photo
illustrates the important identifying characteristics of a striped marlin
that distinguish it from blue and black marlin and also supports the text
that contains Hemingway's theories on the different marlin species.[10]
According to George Reiger,

> Hemingway's 26 page thesis on marlin fishing is less a manual on
> how to catch the fish than a complete natural history of their breed-
> ing habits, migration patterns, and incidental peculiarities. . . . The
> text of "Marlin Off Cuba" is instructive reading for today's students
> of maritime science. The thoroughness of Hemingway's research, and
> the variety and interest of details couched in his lucid prose, make this

chapter one of the most satisfying monographs ever written on a fish. Ultimately, "Marlin Off Cuba" is Hemingway's most notable offering to the memory of Louis Agassiz and his own naturalist father. (255)

Significantly, the thesis also demonstrates how Hemingway's contact with the Gulf Stream was transforming him as a writer and thinker. When set against the transcribed interview with Carlos Gutierrez from July 14, 1932, the reasoned thoroughness of Hemingway's marlin theories becomes more impressive. With the detailed observations of his logs supporting them, the theories convincingly demonstrate how quickly—and how deeply—Hemingway was learning about the Gulf Stream.

Importantly, too, in elaborating on his theories of marlin in his essays again and again, Hemingway translated his observations into precise, representational prose, rendering what he saw without elaboration. The essays in *Esquire* and in *American Big Game Fishing* prove how all the writing Hemingway did—journalism, fiction, and the fishing logs—was overlapping at this time. In "Marlin Off the Morro," Hemingway wrote:

> But the prevailing wind is the north-east trade and when this blows the marlin come to the top and cruise with the wind, scythe tail, a light, steely lavender, cutting the swells as it projects and goes under; the big fish, yellow-looking in the water, swimming two or three feet under the surface, the huge pectoral fins tucked close to the flanks, the dorsal fin down, the fish looking a round, *fast moving log* in the water except for the erect curve of that slicing tail. (141, emphasis added)

The description seems to have been lifted from the fishing logs. The image of the log reappears almost verbatim in "Marlin Off Cuba": "the big fish, yellow looking in the water, swimming two or three feet under the surface, the huge pectoral fins tucked close to the flanks, the dorsal fin down, the fish looking a round fast moving log in the water except for the erect curve of that slicing tail" (57). Hemingway then reused the image of the marlin as a log in *To Have and Have Not*, writing: "Then he came out again and smashed the water white and I could see he was hooked in the side of the mouth. The stripes showed clear on him. He was a fine fish bright silver now, barred with purple, and as big around as a log" (16). Other examples exist, too, as the language of the August 1934 *Esquire* essay overlaps with the description of a marlin's "wagging" in *To Have and Have Not*. In the essay, Hemingway wrote:

He can see the slicing wake of a fin, if he cuts toward the bait, or the rising and lowering sickly of a tail if he is travelling, or if he comes from behind he can see the bulk of him under water, the great blue pectorals widespread like the wings of some huge, underwater bird, and the stripes around him like purple bands around a brown barrel, and then the sudden upthrust waggle of a bill. ("Out in the Stream" 171)

The passage in *To Have and Have Not* reads: "He came on like a submarine and his top fin came out and you could see it slice the water. Then he came right behind the bait and his spear came out too, sort of wagging, clean out of the water" (15). Hemingway had now learned enough about the Gulf Stream to store up material on breeding habits, migration patterns, and fishing techniques that would gestate until the composition of *The Old Man and the Sea*. It was the method of writing that also would come to its fulfillment in the novella published in 1952.

Perhaps still stung by criticism of *Death in the Afternoon* and early responses to *Green Hills of Africa*, Hemingway also presented his most elaborate definition of sport in "Marlin Off Cuba":

As I see big-game fishing with rod and reel it is a sport in which a man or woman seeks to kill or capture a fish by the means which will afford the fisherman the greatest pleasure and best demonstrate the speed, strength and leaping ability of the fish in question; at the same time killing or capturing the fish in the shortest time possible and never for the sake of flattering the fisherman's vanity, using tackle unsuitable to the prompt capture of the fish. I believe that it is as bad to lose fish by breaking unsuitable tackle in an attempt to make a light tackle record as it is to allow animals to escape wounded in an attempt to get a record bag or a record head. Talk of giving the fish a sporting chance on excessively fragile tackle seems nonsense when one realizes that the sporting chance offered the fish is that of breaking the line and going off to die. The sporting thing is to kill your fish as promptly as possible on suitable tackle which does not prevent him running or pulling or jumping to the best of his ability, while you fight him as rapidly as possible to kill him as quickly and mercifully as possible. (70)

As Hemingway spent more and more time on the Gulf Stream, he came in more intimate contact with members of the sporting class, such as

Michael Lerner, S. Kip Farrington, Zane Gray, Dick Cooper, Tommy Shevlin, and Winston Guest. Competing against each other and sharing a common interest in record keeping and conservation, they recognized the need to create a formal organization. A small circle of big game fishermen finally put together a governing body called the Bahamas Marlin and Tuna Club on November 23, 1936.[11] In an article in the *New York City World Telegram*, Ray Trullinger wrote:

> Another new big fish angler's club has just bloomed in our midst, and judging from the eligibility requirements, it doesn't appear the Membership Committee ever will be snowed under with applications. . . . Officers of the new club include Ernest Hemingway, president; Michael Lerner, Thomas Shevlin and A.O.H. Baldridge, vice presidents; Julio Sanchez, treasurer; and Erl Roman, historian.[12]

According to Trullinger, the noteworthy rules were: "1. All fish must be hooked, fought, and brought to gaff by the angler unaided. 6. A mako shark is considered a game fish and should be gaffed and tail-roped. A mako may not be killed by any means other than a club." As an officer of the club, which would evolve into the International Game Fish Association, Hemingway was now ineligible to hold fishing records.[13] Hemingway would serve as vice president of the IGFA from 1940 until his death in 1961. From its earliest days the organization and the American Museum of Natural History had close ties, which were forged by Hemingway. Francesca LaMonte, an associate curator of fish for the museum, served as secretary and as trustee until her retirement in 1978.[14]

Hemingway's own dedication to the IGFA was demonstrated on his only trip to Hawaii in February 1941. Hemingway was sent to the Big Island to investigate a possible world-record catch of a black marlin off the Kona coast by Charles Clapp, a tourist from California.[15] On his return to Havana, Hemingway wrote to LaMonte:

> The Clapp catch used a fishing chair built something like a rowing seat. The rod butt was in a socket which was a part of the chair of which could be rolled back and forth by the attendant. Being attached to the chair the pull of the fish would pull the chair and rod forward. The guard or attendant would then pull the back of the chair back thus gaining line on the fish which the angler would only need to recover by turning the handle on the reel. The entire fishing device was

designed to make it possible for anglers who had never fished before to catch big fish without being subjected to any strain on any part of their bodies except their reeling hand. . . . It is very possible that an affidavit [that the fish was legally caught] was filled out and rushed through. Tourist associations and others interested want to claim a large record fish for Hawaii but my impression in Hawaii was that everyone was disgusted with Finlayson's lack of ethics and honesty in fishing and wished that he had fished honestly and ethically in order that Hawaii might have had a record fish instead of a fish which we must obviously discard as having been caught by unethical methods.

Deeply offended, Hemingway concluded that "there was no possible question about the fish being legally caught." The methods that Clapp had used disqualified him, and the island of Hawaii, from claiming the marlin as a record catch. For efforts such as this, Hemingway was inducted in the IGFA Hall of Fame in January 2000.

The final component of Hemingway's education in the complexities of the Gulf Stream involved patiently assembling a library, as the active life on the *Pilar* had to be supplemented by a thorough reading list. By reviewing James Brasch and Joseph Sigman's *Hemingway's Library: A Composite Record*, I have created a listing of books that may shed light on the composition of *To Have and Have Not* and *The Old Man and the Sea* (see Appendix B). Not included are the books on hunting in Africa, of which there are well over a hundred, or the books on the American West. Both topics influenced Hemingway's thoughts on the Gulf Stream. The first two titles—Wilfrid Alexander's *Birds of the Ocean: A Handbook for Voyagers Containing Descriptions of All the Sea-Birds of the World, with Notes on Their Habits and Guides to Their Identification* and Augusta Arnold's *The Sea-beach at Ebb-Tide: A Guide to the Study of the Seaweeds and the Lower Animal Life Found Between Tidemarks*—indicate the commitment that Hemingway had to learning about the Stream. Neither title represents casual reading. The range of titles related to the Gulf Stream is the index of Hemingway's commitment to learning all he could about his subject; tides, seabirds, seashells, freshwater fish, saltwater fish, conservation, astronomy, whaling, angling, voyaging, and ichthyology are all represented in general and specialized texts. Reviewing the assembled list makes it much clearer what Hemingway meant when he explained his "iceberg principle," stating: "Anything you know you can eliminate, and it only strengthens your story" (Plimpton 125). The library does not reveal what Hemingway actually knew; that is best shown by the complexity of his fiction and nonfiction. Yet writings on fish and fishing in the library do give evidence of the knowledge he valued, and the quantity and breadth of titles demonstrate how much Hemingway felt he needed to know before he could begin "eliminating" material. The culmination of Hemingway's Gulf Stream education is, of course, *The Old Man and the Sea.*

CHAPTER 3

Hemingway's Aesthetics

Cézanne and the "Last Wild Country"

FRONTIER. PASTORAL. Realist. Naturalist. Modernist. The struggle to
define these terms and apply them with clarity to Hemingway is indica-
tive of the broader cultural discord that surrounds labels, as realism,
naturalism, and modernism can be understood as both artistic methods and aesthetic philosophies. Yet in their application to Hemingway,
the terms can become as complex as the man himself, and demand-
ing exclusionary definitiveness denies his multiplicity. In both method
and philosophy he was, at times, a realist, a naturalist, and a modernist. At times, his work creates a frontier and then erodes it. At times,
his worldview is narrow, and then universal. Approaching Hemingway
chronologically organizes these overlaps in his evolving philosophy and
method. Hemingway believed in the authority of his own observations,
and to that end, he always sought to portray the world realistically.
And while at times he was a believer in the church of determinism, he
was also, at times, a conflicted Catholic, and a reluctant patriot. His
complex biography attests to the difficulty of definitively declaring his
belief system. Yet his response to the world was a modern one: an individual was responsible for creating his own meaning through his art
and actions. This interdependency of action and creativity would lead
Hemingway to the Gulf Stream, and his experience would generate the
work of the second half of his life.

By the thirties, Hemingway was no longer describing landscape with
the same techniques he had used for *In Our Time* (1925), *The Sun Also*

When collaborating in the founding of the rules for the International Game Fishing Association, Hemingway continued to be deeply interested in the technology of fishing tackle, insisting that rods and reels be "suitable" to prompt capture of the fish, while also offering it a sporting chance. © Burgert, The John F. Kennedy Library (EH8287P).

A black marlin of twenty-six arrobas would weigh over six hundred pounds and would be celebrated by the whole community of fishermen. This marlin weighed 486 pounds. The John F. Kennedy Library (EH1346P).

Shown here in Havana Harbour in 1932, the *Anita* would serve as the site of Hemingway's initiation into big game fishing and serve as a rough template for his own vessel, *Pilar*. The John F. Kennedy Library (EH1355N).

Following the established ritual of deep documentation, many photos were taken of every significant catch. The John F. Kennedy Library (EH1729N).

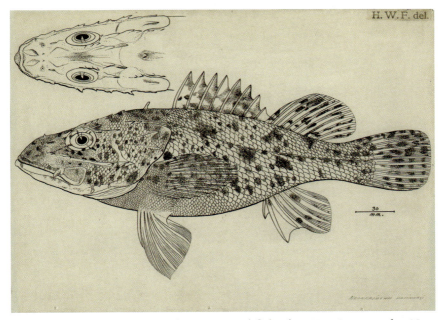

For his efforts, Fowler named a species of fish after Hemingway, the *Neorithe hemingwayi,* stating it was for "Ernest Hemingway, author and angler of great game fishes, in appreciation for his assistance in my work on Gulf Stream fishes" ("New Scorpaenoid" 43). The Academy of Natural Sciences, Ewell Sale Stewart Library.

Hemingway may have been trying to evoke Cézanne's *Rocks in the Forest*, a painting that he stood beside Lillian Ross in 1951, saying: "This is what we try to do in writing, this and this, and woods, and the rocks we have to climb over. . . . Cezanne is my painter." The Metropolitan Museum of Art, H. O. Havemeyer Collection, Bequest of Mrs. H. O. Havemeyer, 1929 (29.100.194). Photograph © 1991 The Metropolitan Museum of Art.

In the color tones, and the perspective of looking over the plain to the mountains, it seems clear that Hemingway was trying to capture the essence of Cézanne's paintings of Mont Sainte-Victoire in Provence. The Metropolitan Museum of Art, The Walter H. and Leonore Annenberg Collection, Gift of Walter H. and Lenore Annenberg, 1994, Bequest of Walter H. Annenberg, 2002 (1994.420). Photograph © 1994 The Metropolitan Museum of Art.

Homer's oil painting *The Gulf Stream* (1899) and his watercolors of the Caribbean served as dual exemplars for Hemingway, as thematically he embraced the former, and in method he embraced the latter. The Metropolitan Museum of Art, Catharine Lorillard Wolfe Collection, Wolfe Fund, 1906 (06.1234). Photograph © 1995 The Metropolitan Museum of Art.

Rises (1926), and *A Farewell to Arms* (1929). As he shifted his attention to the Gulf Stream, his verbal language, too, had to accommodate the new seascape. If Cézanne's impressionism was an appropriate technique to mimic in describing the hills of Spain, the battlefields of Italy, and the deep woods of Michigan, Homer's stark realistic canvases provided a model for his later work.

Hemingway has frequently but uncomfortably been included in the category of American literary naturalists. Yet the terms "naturalist," "realist," and "modernist" all overlap in their application to Hemingway's work, and in their own way, each term shines light on the transformations in his writing. Among the many definitions of "naturalist," at least two apply to Hemingway. A naturalist is, of course, a student of natural history or a field biologist. Secondly, a naturalist is a practitioner of naturalism, which is, according to *Webster's*, "realism in art or literature; *specif:* a theory in literature emphasizing scientific observation of life without idealization or the avoidance of the ugly" (788). Hemingway would have happily embraced being labeled a naturalist, or a marine biologist. Yet he would have resisted being classified as a literary naturalist; to him, the grouping would have delineated a temporary genre that had briefly won the admiration of critics. His ambitions always were grander than that. Still, scholars approaching his work as a whole continue to rigidly place Hemingway within the American naturalist tradition while overlooking his experiments in technique and style, and the growth in his philosophy.[1] The difficulty in affixing labels to Hemingway's writing style results from his continually evolving method of composition. Chronological awareness is essential to understanding his work.

When *A Farewell to Arms* was published to great reviews in 1929, because of his early affiliation with Gertrude Stein, critics were swift to note the "modernist" qualities of his work that seemed to mimic hers. Hemingway's reputation as the leading writer of his generation was solidified, fulfilling the critical promise of *In Our Time* and *The Sun Also Rises*. Critics noticed how the themes and style fulfilled the doctrines of the aesthetics of modernism. According to Daniel Singal,

> The most prevalent view until recently did not see [modernism] as a full-scale historical culture at all but rather equated it with the beliefs and lifestyle of the artistic avante-garde at the turn of the

century. Used in this sense, the term usually connotes radical experimentation in artistic style, a deliberate cultivation of the perverse
and decadent, and the flaunting of outrageous behavior designed to
shock the bourgeoisie. (8)

At this stage in Hemingway's career, Singal's definition would have ap-
plied to his work, as his contemporary Clifton Fadiman called the novel
"the very apotheosis of a kind of modernism" (Baker, *Life* 204). The use
of vignettes in *In Our Time* was clearly an experimentation in form,
just as the drinking and sexual content of *The Sun Also Rises* portrayed
behavior that would "shock the bourgeoisie." As a resident of Paris,
and a friend to figures such as Picasso, James Joyce, and Ezra Pound,
Hemingway was part of a new, modern movement in the arts. Fanny
Butcher of the *Paris Tribune* wrote:

> Ernest Hemingway is the direct blossoming of Gertrude Stein's art.
> Whether he consciously was influenced by her no one, of course, can
> say. But he does in "A Farewell to Arms," what Gertrude Stein did in
> "Three Lives," except that he does it in a longer, more complicated
> medium and with more certain power. There are whole pages in the
> new book which might have been written by Gertrude Stein herself,
> except that even in their most tortuous intricacies, the reader is per-
> fectly clear about what Mr. Hemingway is saying and why he is say-
> ing it that way. (Reynolds, *1930s* 28)

The title, wrote Malcolm Cowley, was symbolic of "Hemingway's
farewell to a period, an attitude, and perhaps to a method also" (Baker,
Life 204). Yet even as *A Farewell to Arms* is seen as a representation of
modernism, it also contains passages that came to epitomize literary
naturalism, as Singal writes: "The Modernist ethos insists on confronting the ugly, the sordid, and the terrible, for that is where the most
important lessons are to be found" (12). Literary naturalism, and the
"Modernist ethos," the former a method and the latter a philosophy,
both turn away from the polite, genteel world to celebrate the unpleas-
ant and contradictory elements of post–World War I society.

Several vital passages of *A Farewell to Arms* are always cited when
it is referred to as a naturalist novel. In book 2, Catherine Barkley tells
Frederic Henry that she is pregnant. Catherine asks Frederic if he feels
trapped in their relationship by her pregnancy. Frederic replies: "You al-

ways feel trapped biologically" (139). Nature, not free will, according to naturalist critics, controls the destiny of this couple. Frederic feels bound not by obligations of religion, society, or family duty, but only by the biological connection he has to the child. In book 4, Hemingway writes:

> If people bring so much courage to this world the world has to kill them to break them, so of course it kills them. The world breaks every one and afterward many are strong at the broken places. But those that will not break it kills. It kills the very good and the very gentle and the very brave impartially. If you are none of these you can be sure it will kill you too but there will be no special hurry. (249)

A Farewell to Arms is a novel written in the past tense, as a remembrance of events that already occurred; this passage foreshadows Catherine's death, underscoring that her personal fortitude is meaningless since biological laws control her fate. The indifference of nature to human suffering serves to heighten the misery of the characters, rendering their individual actions empty of meaning. The final passage frequently cited by critics occurs near the end of the novel, as Catherine's death is imminent, and Frederic feels helpless:

> Once in camp I put a log on top of the fire and it was full of ants. As it commenced to burn, the ants swarmed out and went first toward the centre where the fire was; then turned back and ran toward the end. When there were enough on the end they fell off into the fire. Some got out, their bodies burnt and flattened, and went off not knowing where they were going. But most of them went toward the fire and then back toward the end and swarmed on the cool end and finally fell off into the fire. I remember thinking at the time that it was the end of the world and a splendid chance to be a messiah and lift the log off the fire and throw it out where the ants could get off onto the ground. But I did not do anything but throw a tin cup of water on the log, so that I would have the cup empty to put whiskey in before I added water to it. I think the cup of water on the burning log only steamed the ants. (327–28)

Interpreters cite this passage as emphasizing the futility of individual actions in a "burning" world. Interfering with the course of nature, according to Hemingway, often heightens suffering, rather than alleviating it. Recognizing the impossibility of being a messiah, Frederic's careless gesture, an extension of his own self-interest in preparing his cup for whiskey, creates additional misery.

Hemingway's first generation of critics found in *A Farewell to Arms* ample evidence to support their definitions of literary naturalism. In a 1945 article entitled "The Biological Trap," Ray West wrote:

> This raises the question of Ernest Hemingway's method—his style, Hemingway's sensibility, when it is functioning at its highest point, has always worked upon an immediate objective level which translates ideas into terms of concrete things: life as a baseball game where each error is punished by death or compared to the struggle of ants on a burning log, the comparison of a hero's death with the slaughter of animals in a stockyard. In each case we are aware of the double implication, the idea and the image; and the emotional force of the idea is intensified by the shock supplied by the image. This is the more complicated form of Hemingway's noted "understatement." (150)

West recognized how Hemingway's style conforms to literary naturalism: by selectively using nature as an exemplar of man's condition, and by not interpreting that example, Hemingway creates the effect of understatement. In his 1956 work *American Literary Naturalism, A Divided Stream,* Charles Walcutt wrote:

> [Hemingway's] early works struggle continually against the fact that modern public morality, having lost touch with the facts of life, reveals a corrupt and despicable travesty of idealism. In them the very concept of idealism is eschewed because it has been so badly mauled that Hemingway will have nothing to do with it, while he concentrates on establishing certain definite, tangible, basic areas of expertise that he can treat without being contaminated by the prevailing hypocrisy of his time. (271)

The natural world, according to Walcutt, provided an uncontaminated landscape by which to illustrate the corruption of a civilization without idealism. Hemingway's protagonists must create their own meaning by cultivating their own world of meaning through fishing, bullfights, and athletics. As Paul Civello wrote thirty-eight years later, "Hemingway, in assimilating this modern view of humanity into his work would transform the naturalistic novel by depicting a distinctly modern response—one in which the self creates its own order and meaning—to the naturalistic world of force" (67).

Yet scholars still struggle to define naturalism and to apply it to Hemingway. John Conder wrote in 1984: "It is now clear that no critical consensus exists to explain the commonly used term literary naturalism as distinct from literary realism" (1). Donald Pizer, attempting clarification, wrote: "Naturalism, is above all, social realism laced with the idea of determinism" (14). Sidney Gendin, challenging the existence of a distinct method for naturalism, tried to define it in 1995:

> 1. Realism: a method of composition by which the author describes normal, average life in an accurate truthful way. 2. Naturalism: a method of composition by which an author portrays life as it is in accordance with the philosophic theory of determinism. Such authors believe men lack free will. (90)

The first component of Gendin's definition of realism would apply to *To Have and Have Not*. Realism, according to David Shi, means intellectual and artistic honesty rather than romantic exaggeration, involving a direct confrontation with life, rather than an art-for-art's-sake aestheticism (5). Shi continues:

> What all realists held in common was a language of rebellion against the genteel elite governing American taste. They predominately invoked such terms as "sentimental," "romantic," artificial," "anachronistic," and "effeminate" to express their disdain for the prevailing modes of idealism dominating thought and expression. Threaded together more by such oppositional discourse than by a uniform creed, realists could communicate with and applaud each other, but the very fact that they operated primarily out of a rhetorical rather than a philosophical framework allowed them a marked degree of independence from one another. (6)

Hemingway would have agreed with that. Yet declaring Hemingway an adherent to determinism is problematic. His most deterministic novels are clearly *A Farewell to Arms* and *To Have and Have Not*. In the former, he is more of an impressionist in method and a naturalist in philosophy, while in the latter, Gendin's definition seems to fit. Determinism controls the fate of Harry Morgan, and the novel is devoid of moral judgments. To many of his characters in other novels, however—notably Jake Barnes, Robert Jordan, and Santiago—the possibilities of free will provide the drama of the narrative, and Gendin's definition is a sloppy fit.

In his 1998 book *The Urban Sublime in American Literary Naturalism*, Christophe Den Tandt sought to update the classification of literature that was done by earlier scholars. Addressing Hemingway, he writes:

> The stylistic terseness of writers like Hemingway, the dislocation of their speech into apparently self-contained fragments, stands as the dialectic counterpart of the sprawling romantic cadences of the naturalist idiom. Hemingway's discontinuous prose, for instance, represses any upsurge of the romantic idiom of earlier sociologically oriented literature. This aesthetic asceticism is predicated on the belief that literature can do without the world—or at least without the world in the sense of a social scene broad enough to stand as a metaphor of a totality of human activities. (244)

To Den Tandt, Hemingway is not a literary naturalist; his "terseness" runs contrary to a documentary impulse within naturalism to that surge into a florid, romantic idiom. From the broad nature of his remarks, it is clear that Den Tandt has not read Hemingway closely, as there are passages of Joycean inner monologues in *To Have and Have Not* and *For Whom the Bell Tolls* (1940) that flow with emotion and a romantic hunger for what has been lost. The short, declarative sentences that predominate in Hemingway's early style are most notable in the dialogue in his short fiction, and they begin to disappear after *To Have and Have Not*. While Hemingway ascribed to "aesthetic asceticism"—he clearly believed that less language gave more emotion to the reader—he did not believe that literature could do without the world. As sections of *Green Hills of Africa* and *The Old Man and the Sea* attest, Hemingway was quite capable of creating metaphors for a "totality of human activities."

It is important to note, too, that Hemingway never declared himself a naturalist, a realist, or a modernist. Immodestly, he would insist on the uniqueness of his own talent, declaring it as original as Shakespeare's. Hemingway would also insist on the uniqueness of American literature, as he famously declared *Huckleberry Finn* its source:

> All modern American literature comes from one book by Mark Twain called *Huckleberry Finn*. If you read it you must stop where

the Nigger Jim is stolen from the boys. That is the real end. The rest is just cheating. But it's the best book we've had. All American writing comes from that. There was nothing before. There has been nothing as good since. (*Green Hills of Africa* 22)

What Hemingway admired in Twain was the use of the vernacular, the authentic voice of a child, to tell his story. Hemingway placed this comment in *Green Hills of Africa,* the book that contains his most direct exploration of the regenerative power of the Gulf Stream. As Bert Bender notes, as Twain responded to the Mississippi, so Hemingway responded to the Gulf Stream (171). With Twain, Cooper, Melville, and Crane as his models, Hemingway could not allow himself to be grouped into a broad category of writers that included his friend John Dos Passos, James T. Farrell, Frank Norris, and Upton Sinclair. Hemingway could not be a naturalist, in his view, because it diminished the trajectory of his talent and tainted him by associating him with writers he considered inferior. In order to place himself in his own category, Hemingway began talking about writing as a form of painting, and following his apprenticeship with Gertrude Stein, there was no greater painter than Paul Cézanne.

Indeed, the aesthetic of those canvases that he had viewed at Stein's would shape Hemingway's emergent aesthetics of writing from 1924 to 1929. Thus, in a manuscript fragment from "Big Two-Hearted River" composed in August 1924, he would write:

He wanted to write like Cezanne painted. Cezanne started with all the tricks. Then he broke the whole thing down and built the real thing. It was hell to do. He was the greatest. The greatest for always. It wasn't a cult. He, Nick, wanted to write about country so it would be there like Cezanne had done it in painting. You had to do it from inside yourself. There wasn't any trick. Nobody had ever written about country like that. You could do it if you could fight it out. *If you lived with your eyes.* It was a thing you couldn't talk about. He was going to work on it until he got it. Maybe never. It was a job. Maybe for all his life. . . . He knew just how Cezanne would paint this stretch of river. God, if he were only here to do it. They died and that was the hell of it. They worked all their lives and then got old and died. *Nick, seeing how Cezanne would do the stretch of river and the swamp, stood up and stepped down into the stream. The water was cold and actual.* ("On Writing" 239, emphasis added)

Indeed, eight years before introducing his iceberg principle of writing—initiating the next phase of his aesthetics—Hemingway wrote this passage in celebration of Cézanne. Hemingway may have been trying to evoke Cézanne's *Rocks in the Forest,* a painting that he stood beside Lillian Ross in 1951, saying: "This is what we try to do in writing, this and this, and woods, and the rocks we have to climb over. . . . Cezanne is my painter" (Ross 87; see figure 6). Prior to his immersion in the world of the Gulf Stream, the painting analogy is the best tool for understanding how Hemingway created passages describing the landscape. The language that applies to painting corresponds to the language used to describe Hemingway's writing, but the parallels should be understood as evocative, rather than a precise correlation. Cézanne and Homer are painters who represented Hemingway's aesthetic inclinations before and after his contact with the Gulf Stream.[2] To say that he learned to "write like Cezanne painted" added an element of polish and mystery to his method, creating an ambiguity in his art that defied easy categorization. Hemingway systematically sought to transform what he saw into verbal canvases that were spare, elemental, and emotionally condensed. In a September 12, 1924, letter to his first editor, Edward O'Brien, Hemingway again articulated the effect for which he was striving. He wrote:

> Some of the stories I think you would like very much. I wish I could show them to you. The last one in the book is called Big Two Hearted River, it is about 12,000 words and goes back after a ski-ing [sic] story and My Old Man and finishes up the Michigan scene the book starts with. It is much better than anything I have done. What I've been doing is trying to do country so you don't remember the words after you read it but actually have the Country. It is hard to do because to do it you have to see the country all complete all the time you write and not just have a romantic feeling about it. It is swell fun. (*Selected Letters* 123)

The ambition of giving the "Country" over to the reader through his descriptions is an idea that Hemingway would return to again when he began to write about the Gulf Stream. Related to his belief in the authority of facts, Hemingway felt that if he were severely honest in his descriptions, something almost magical would happen as the reader received his words: he could give the reader his experience. With an aspiration this grand, it is no wonder that Hemingway resisted being grouped with the literary naturalists.

Once more, *A Farewell to Arms* became the text that critics would use to make declarations about Hemingway's painterly method. Uniformly, the critics begin by examining the first paragraph of the novel:

> In the late summer of that year we lived in a house in a village that looked across the river and the plain to the mountains. In the bed of the river there were pebbles and boulders, dry and white in the sun, and the water was clear and swiftly moving and blue in the channels. Troops went by the house and down the road and the dust they raised powdered the leaves of the trees. The trunks of the trees too were dusty and the leaves fell early that year and we saw the troops marching along the road and the dust rising and leaves, stirred by the breeze falling and the soldiers marching and afterward the road bare and white except for the leaves. (3)

The contrasting textures of the dry leaves and the swiftly moving river, the repetition of the words "leaves," "dust," and "white," and the movement of the troops through the carefully described setting—these elements would become the essential components of a Hemingway imitation. In the color tones, and the perspective of looking over the plain to the mountains, it seems clear that Hemingway was trying to capture the essence of Cézanne's paintings of Mont Sainte-Victoire in Provence. Cézanne's principle of "flat depth" seems to have enthralled Hemingway, as he, like Cézanne, is trying to simultaneously create a sense of deep space within flatness. Most important for the purpose of understanding how his aesthetics shift is that Hemingway is showing the reader what is there, on the surface; this is a portrayal of what things looked like, rather than what is below the surface. The different textures of the elements—the swiftly moving water and the dry dust—accentuate their separateness and the disturbance of nature's cycles due to the war.

Even Hemingway's reluctant admirers noted the paragraph's affinity to Cézanne. In a 1977 cover story for the *New Republic* entitled "Hemingway, the Painter," Alfred Kazin wrote:

> Painting far more than writing suggests the actual texture of human happiness. Hemingway understood that; what excited him as a writer

about painting was a promise of relief from civilization, a touch of the promised land. (26)

After interpreting Hemingway in these pastoral terms, Kazin continued:

If Cezanne's greatness lay in the removal of his subjects from the contingent world, this opening paragraph is an imitation of that removal. It is exclusively an impression from the outside, it rests with the eye of the beholder. As an impression it is static, for it calls attention to the beholder's effort to capture one detail after another rather than to the scene of the war. As so often happens in Hemingway's prose forays into war, bullfighting, marlin fishing, hunting, there is an unnatural pause in the last sentence—"leaves stirred by the breeze"—a forced transition made necessary by "painting" the scene in words. We positively see the writer at his easel. (26)

Thus, according to Kazin, the repetition in the language serves as the underpinnings of the scene, establishing the frame of the natural world and illustrating what Hemingway wrote in *Death in the Afternoon* (1932): "Prose is architecture, not interior decoration" (191). In a 1987 interview, Derek Walcott echoed Kazin's appreciation:

A passage I always quote when I'm teaching is the first chapter of *A Farewell to Arms* in which the model is really a combination of Gertrude Stein and Cezanne [*sic*]. Sometimes I point out to the class certain effects Hemingway achieved by watching Cezanne. One was to let the stroke of the word "blue" appear very late in the first paragraphs. So that the first startling stroke of the word "blue" comes much later, after the dust and the leaves and so on, and waters swiftly moving are blue in the channels. Now *what* blue is not described, but the point is that the stroke is put down with exactly the same cubic area that a Cezanne stroke is put on a bleached background. Or say the rocks or trees are skeletally or sparingly indicated, and then that stroke appeared next to another hue—a blue or a lilac, and so on. (Montenegro 137–38)

Yet as rich and provocative as these analogies are, what the Cézanne comparison actually does is encapsulate Hemingway in a style and in a period, declaring him a writer with a static approach to his craft forever the pupil of Gertrude Stein. Perhaps recognizing that as long as he dwelled publicly in the fuzzy zone between writing and painting he would infuse his method with an aura of mystery, Hemingway never renounced the comparison.

Yet Hemingway's formula for writing had changed by 1952. In the initial description of the Gulf Stream in *The Old Man and the Sea*, Hemingway wrote:

> The old man knew he was going far out and he left the smell of the land behind and rowed out into the clean early morning smell of the ocean. He saw the phosphorescence of the Gulf weed in the water as he rowed over the part of the ocean that the fisherman called the great well because there was a sudden deep of seven hundred fathoms where all sorts of fish congregated because of the swirl the current made against the steep walls of the floor of the ocean. Here were concentrations of shrimp and bait fish and sometimes schools of squid in the deepest holes and these rose close to the surface at night where all the wandering fish fed on them. (28–29)

Hemingway's precise language describes the observed world of the Stream, directly classifying the marine life. Like Winslow Homer's brushstrokes, each word is representational, establishing order within the natural world, equal to the compositional order of a canvas. Repetition and contrasting textures are abandoned, and Hemingway is no longer using shapes and colors to convey meaning indirectly.

But the main difference between this passage and the beginning of *A Farewell to Arms* is that in *The Old Man and the Sea*, Santiago is aware of what is beneath the surface of the ocean. He has studied the Gulf Stream, and he is aware of the organic unity that exists within nature. My hypothesis is that the shift in Hemingway's writing method is a result of the hundreds of days he had spent on the Gulf Stream from 1932 to 1952, creating short representational phrases to record what he saw, learning from his observations, and using that knowledge later in his fiction. For example, on May 17, 1932, Hemingway recorded:

> Hooked Marlin opposite Cojimar 2 jumps threw hook—930 swam at beach 3pm—saw first big striped marlin tail at least three feet behind teaser deep down
> —Back a foot or more across

came to surface and when we
curled boat but [illegible] down before
we saw baits (sky was very overcast) and had
strike from another marlin.

Hemingway is trying to create an objective document representing unadorned what he observed in a narrative that uses precise descriptive
phrases—"big striped marlin tail at least three feet"—in order to see exactly the world of the Gulf Stream. Hemingway connects the behavior
of the marlin with the overcast sky to understand their interdependence
in a way that will be essential to Santiago's narration. In the fishing
logs, Hemingway is learning what exists beneath the iceberg.

And while there can be no doubt that there is a transformation in
Hemingway's writing style, I recognize, too, that from the beginning,
he was basing his narratives on what actually happened. He never fully
abandoned the architectural devices he used in *A Farewell to Arms* and
his earlier short stories. But there is a shift in emphasis on the devices
that Hemingway uses that occurs in *The Old Man and the Sea*, which
could be attributed to the intense daily observations inscribed in the
fishing logs, allowing him to create more representational narratives.

Indeed, the evolutionary nature of Hemingway's thinking about the
Gulf Stream and the natural world is revealed through close examination
of *To Have and Have Not* and *The Old Man and the Sea*. The passage
of time is crucial to this transformation in thinking and writing technique.[3] Hemingway's changes, like the movement of an iceberg, are slow.
To Have and Have Not was published in 1937, yet the first section of
the novel was published as "One Trip Across" in *Cosmopolitan* in 1934.
Hemingway began fishing the Gulf Stream in earnest in 1931. The first
of his elaborate fishing logs was created then, and logs exist from 1932,
1934, 1936, and 1939. The transformation in Hemingway's worldview
and the related shift in his writing technique would not fully manifest
themselves until the completion of *The Old Man and the Sea* in 1952.

Literary Naturalism on the Stream

To Have and Have Not

WHEN DID HEMINGWAY begin writing "One Trip Across," the first section of *To Have and Have Not*, which would be published in 1937? Available evidence is inconclusive. On February 23, 1933, he wrote Max Perkins: "Am on Chapter 4 of the novel—going well. See my way all the way to the end. Don't know whether we ever talked about this one" (*Only Thing* 183). In a March 13 letter, Hemingway asks Perkins for a letter "certify[ing] that Ernest Hemingway is at work on a book dealing with the migratory fish of the Gulf Stream, their habits and capture with special reference to the fishing in Cuban Waters from a sporting standpoint" in order to get him out of any possible "jams" in Cuba (*Only Thing* 184). The chronology of locations is straightforward: from April 13 to July 20, Hemingway was in Havana fishing for marlin from the *Anita* (Baker, *Life* 244). He then spent July 21 to August 3 in Key West, preparing for his departure to Europe and Africa. He returned to Havana on August 4, and on the seventh, he left Havana for Spain, where he would be through October. Carlos Baker asserts that Hemingway began the story sometime in April (Baker, *Life* 607), but Michael Reynolds believes that the story was begun in Madrid on September 22 (Reynolds, *The 1930s* 146). From Madrid on October 16, Hemingway wrote his mother-in-law a long report on his new fiction:

It is almost a third as long as the average novel. It may be a very good story. It is almost entirely action and takes place in Cuba and on the sea. Plenty of action. It is exactly the story that this present book needs i.e. Winner Take Nothing. But it will be as well or better in another book. You can't very well put a story that you know will sell like hotcakes in a book called Winner Take Nothing. I don't expect anyone to like the present book of stories and don't think you have to make an effort to—or even be polite about them. *I am trying to make, before I get through, a picture of the whole world—or as much of it as I have seen. Boiling it down always, rather than spreading it thin.* These stories are about things and people that people won't care about—or will actively dislike. All right. Sooner or later as the wheel keeps turning I will have ones they will like. (*Selected Letters* 397, emphasis added)

Especially noteworthy is the language that he uses to describe his method at this point: "mak[ing] . . . a picture of the whole world," "boiling it down always." More directly than anywhere else in his writing, this is Hemingway's declaration of a writing method that was an approximation of literary naturalism. There is the documentary impulse to "make . . . a picture of the whole world," yet also the imperative that he "boil" down that picture to its most primitive, essential elements. Clearly, the story Hemingway refers to here is "One Trip Across," which would be finished in mid-September and published in *Cosmopolitan* the following April (Baker, *Life* 607).

And although two questions can never fully be resolved—on what day did Hemingway begin "One Trip Across," and did he have his fishing log from the *Anita* beside him to spur his imagination?—what is certain is that Hemingway almost instantly began fictionalizing his personal experience fishing the Gulf Stream. While it had taken nearly ten years for the events that formed the core of *A Farewell to Arms* to gestate in his imagination and resurface in fiction, Hemingway was wasting no time in reimagining and transforming his initiation into big game fishing into the realist narrative of Harry Morgan, a fishing guide witnessing Cuba on the brink of revolution.

There has always been the tendency to read Hemingway's fiction autobiographically and to understand his characters as surrogates for Hemingway the writer. As Rose Marie Burwell writes, "Hemingway's heroes had always been fictional visions of himself, but they were also demonstrably other than himself, so that fictional distance protected the author" (5). No other Hemingway character demonstrates this impulse toward negative autobiographical interpretations better than Harry

Morgan, the protagonist of *To Have and Have Not*. There is much to dislike about Morgan, and if you attribute his racism, cruelty, and self-ishness to Hemingway, then the writer becomes a despicable person.[1] However, Hemingway is trying to create the world as experienced by Morgan, and all the ugliness in that character should be understood as an attempt to portray authentically a narrative point of view.[2]

In the first pages of the novel, it becomes clear that Morgan must respond heroically to the challenges of his environment. Opening with a frontier-style shootout in a Havana café, Hemingway establishes three distinct stages for Morgan, his proletarian hero. Havana is a wide-open town, devoid of law and order; shootouts are common, and retribution is swift. Key West is a despoiled Eden, a microcosm of America during the Depression, where distasteful tourism is a palliative for deeper economic and moral troubles. In *The Idea of Florida in the American Literary Imagination*, Anne Rowe writes: "The land is raped in the sense that a pastoral setting will now be exploited as hordes of greedy profit seekers pour in" (24). Key West has been a holdout against bourgeois American life. Once Key West is contaminated by the bourgeois mentality, Morgan is forced out into the Gulf Stream. The Gulf Stream between Key West and Havana thus becomes a no-man's-land, a contested space where violence settles disputes in the midst of an indifferent natural world.

Hemingway's first description of the Gulf Stream appears as Morgan is taking a tourist, Mr. Johnson, out fishing for marlin:

> The stream was in almost to soundings and as we came toward the edge you could see her running purple with regular whirlpools. There was a slight east breeze coming up and we put up plenty of flying fish, those big ones with the black wings that look like the picture of Lind-bergh crossing the Atlantic when they sail off. Those big flying fish are the best sign there is. As far as you could see, there was that faded gulf-weed in small patches that means the stream is well in and there are birds ahead working over a school of little tuna. You could see them jumping; just little ones weighing a couple of pounds a piece. (12)

Hemingway is writing in the voice of Morgan, a member of the working class, and his observations are matter of fact, creating not a lyrical, literary description but instead an extension of a fishing log. Locations, wind direction, tide color, and animal life are all worth commenting on, and the most descriptive moment—the picture of Lindbergh crossing the

Atlantic—seems an appropriate popular culture reference from the mind of a narrator nurtured on the mass media. Even in noting the weight of the tuna, Morgan is making a practical rather than lyrical observation; the tuna exist as an economic resource for him, and these small ones are not worth harvesting.

Scenes with enormous fighting marlin appear twice early in the novel, allowing Hemingway to reveal Morgan's expertise as a fisherman. Hemingway's descriptions are direct, rich in color, and active. Johnson, Morgan's customer, is fishing for marlin along the Cuban coast near Havana. Hemingway writes:

> I opened the bottle and was reaching it toward him when I saw this big brown buggar with a spear on him longer than your arm burst head and shoulders out of the water and smash that mackerel. He looked as big around as a saw log. . . . You could see his fins out wide like purple wings and the purple stripes across the brown. He came on like a submarine and his top fin came out and you could see it slice the water. . . . He hit him pretty hard a couple times more, and then the rod bent double and the reel commenced to screech and out he came, boom, in a long straight jump, shining silver in the sun and making a splash like throwing a horse off a cliff. . . . He was a fine fish bright silver now, barred with purple, and as big around as a log. . . . Then once, twice, he came out stiff as a post, the whole length of him jumping straight toward us, throwing the water high each time he landed. The line came taut and I saw he was headed inshore again and I could see he was turning. . . . The old marlin headed out to the nor'west like all the big ones go, and brother, did he hook up. . . . I kept yelling to Johnson to keep his drag light and reel fast. All of the sudden I see his rod jerk and the line go slack. . . . "He's gone," I told him. (15–17)

The colors of the fish ("bright silver"), the dynamism of the movements, the excitement of the battle—Hemingway is letting the reader know that he is an expert fisherman. Deep-sea fishing, like herding cattle or hunting big game, is an endeavor that needs to be trusted to seasoned experts who know the Gulf Stream.

Hemingway lets his urban outsider get another chance at a marlin, as several pages later, Johnson hooks into the "biggest black marlin [Morgan] ever saw" (19). Morgan, an expert watching a novice blunder, continues his narration:

I was at the wheel and was working the edge of the stream opposite that old cement factory where it makes deep so close in to shore and where it makes a sort of eddy where there is always lots of bait. Then I saw a splash like a depth bomb, and the sword, and eye, and open lower-jaw and huge purple-black head of a black marlin. The whole top fin was up out of the water looking as high as a full rigged ship, and the whole scythe tail was out as he smashed at that tuna. The bill was as big around as a baseball bat and slanted up, and as he grabbed the bait he sliced the ocean wide open. He was solid purple-black and he had an eye as big as a soup bowl. He was huge. I bet he'd go a thousand pounds. I yelled to Johnson to let him have line but before I could say a word, I saw Johnson rise up in the air off the chair as though he was being derricked, and him holding just for a second onto that rod and the rod bending like a bow, and then the butt caught him in the belly and the whole works went overboard. He'd screwed the drag tight, and when the fish struck, it lifted Johnson right out of the chair and he couldn't hold it. . . . "What was it?" he said to me. "Black marlin," I said. (20–21)

Johnson's incompetence, his ignorance of the remarkable fish, and his remorseless loss of the fishing rod all signal him as a naive urban outsider in a frontier world. The clipped two-word reply of Morgan to Johnson's question underscores the disgust he feels at Johnson's behavior, as well as his anger at a universe that is so unfair as to let Johnson hook a spectacular thousand-pound marlin. Notable, too, is the passive observation of Morgan in this scene, and the one before it. Morgan offers advice; Johnson ignores it, disrespecting his expertise. As men from separate worlds—Morgan, a man of the outdoors and the Gulf Stream, and Johnson, a man of the city—they are separated by a boundary that prevents them from effectively communicating. Morgan derives a certain satisfaction in watching Johnson's humiliation.

As chapter 3 begins, Morgan is leaving Havana to pick up Chinese refugees to smuggle into Key West. The description of the departure is noteworthy as an example of the concrete, matter-of-fact vision appropriate to a naturalistic novel. Morgan narrates:

I went out the harbor and past the Morro and put her on the course for Key West due north. . . . I dropped the Morro out of sight after a while and then the National Hotel and finally I could just see the dome of the Capitol. There wasn't much current compared to the last day we had fished and there was only a light breeze. I saw a couple of smacks headed toward Havana and they were coming from the westward, so I knew the current was light. I cut the switch and killed the motor. There wasn't any sense in wasting gas. I let her drift. When it got dark I could always pick up the light of the Morro or, if she drifted too far, the lights of Cojimar, and steer in and run along to Barcuranao. I figured the way the current looked she would drift the twelve miles up to Barcuranao by dark and I'd see the lights of Baracoa. . . . All there was to see was the two smacks off to the westward headed in, and way back the dome of the Capitol standing up white out of the edge of the sea. . . . I sat up there awhile on top of the house and watched but the only fish I saw were those little brown ones that use around [sic] the gulfweed. Brother, don't let anybody tell you there isn't plenty of water between Havana and Key West. I was just on the edge of it. (42–43)

This long passage describing the activity of the Gulf Stream stands in opposition to the long passage in *Green Hills of Africa* describing the same stretch of coastline, explored earlier. Here the emphasis is on the visible world, what can be seen by Morgan, and landmarks of the Havana coastline are listed. The effects of the weather, the stars, the clouds, and the marine life go unmentioned. The Gulf Stream, for Morgan, is a highway and a resource, not a symbol, and Hemingway, like his narrator, is just beginning to learn about its complexity.

When Morgan arrives in Key West a day later, a confrontation worthy of a John Ford Western has taken place. After picking up the Chinese refugees, Morgan brutally kills the smuggler, Mr. Sing, breaking his neck as he "flopped like a fish" (53). Morgan forces the twelve Chinese refugees to jump overboard in the cove of Bacuranao, still in Cuba. Pleased and remorseless, Morgan savors the $1,200 he has pocketed as he arrives in Key West:

Then we came to the edge of the stream and the water quit being blue and was light and greenish inside I could see the stakes on the Eastern and Western Dry Rocks and the wireless masts at Key West and La Concha hotel up high out of all the low houses and plenty smoke from where they're burning garbage. Sand Key light was plenty close now and you could see the boathouse and the little dock alongside the light and I knew we were only forty minutes away now and I felt good to be getting back and I had a good stake now for the summertime. (61)

As Morgan and Eddie, his alcoholic mate, travel this distance in silence, Jane Tompkins notes not talking is a demonstration of masculine control over emotion, their silence symbolizing a massive suppression of their inner life (66). The landscape of the Western, silent, impenetrable, allows the John Wayne heroes to be silent as well. Thus, the silence of Morgan and the uncomplicated nature of his "good" feeling can be understood as an extension of this silent seascape.

As the victor of the gunfight of part 1, Morgan's luck would turn in part 2 when he loses his arm while smuggling liquor. In part 3 he would be found lying on the deck of his boat, shot in the stomach by Cuban revolutionaries. The narrative point of view has shifted to third-person omniscient. Although the passage is long, it will be quoted in its entirety in order to demonstrate Hemingway's attempt to use the Gulf Stream symbolically in a way that foreshadows *The Old Man and the Sea*. Placing Morgan ten miles out in the Gulf Stream water, Hemingway writes:

There was no sign of life on her although the body of a man showed, rather inflated looking, above the gunwale, lying on a bench over the port gasoline tank and from the long seat alongside the starboard gunwale, a man seemed to be leaning over to dip his hand into the sea. His head and arms were in the sun and at the point where his fingers almost touched the water there was a school of small fish, about two inches long, oval-shaped, golden-colored, with faint purple stripes, that had deserted the gulf weed to take shelter in the shade the bottom of the drifting launch made in the water, and each time anything dripped down into the sea, these fish rushed at the drop and pushed and milled until it was gone. . . . They were reluctant now to leave a place where they had fed so well and unexpectedly. . . . The launch had been drifting since 10 o'clock of the night before and it was now getting late in the afternoon. There was nothing else in sight across the surface of the Gulf Stream but the gulf weed, a few pink, inflated membranous bubbles of Portuguese men-of-war cocked jauntily on the surface, and the distant smoke of a loaded tanker bound north from Tampico. (179–81)

In having the human blood mix with the waters of the Gulf Stream, Hemingway is striving to achieve a unity of what Ray West calls a "double implication," where the emotional force of the idea is intensified by the shock supplied by the image (150). The enduring world of the Gulf Stream is juxtaposed here with the image of a life wasting away. The fish, unable to comprehend the regularity of the drip, parallel the uncomprehending Morgan, who is unaware of the natural laws that control his fate. Combining with the image of the suckerfish, Morgan's "inflated" body becomes an ironic pun on the inflated importance with which he regards himself. Forty pages later, Morgan finally utters his last words:

> "A man," Harry Morgan said, looking at them both. "One man alone ain't got. No man alone now." He stopped. "No matter how a man alone ain't got no bloody fucking chance." He shut his eyes. It had taken him a long time to get it out and it had taken him all of his life to learn it. (225)

Morgan's words are not heard by those around him, underscoring the futility of the knowledge he has acquired; his death was determined by his position in a class-oriented society driven by the laws of nature.[3] Indeed, the Darwinian echoes are accentuated in the final pages of the novel, as the tycoon, Henry Carpenter, tries to fall asleep by reading. Hemingway writes: "He lay, now in his pyjamas, on his wide bed, two pillows under his head, the reading light on, but he could not keep his mind on the book, which was an account of a trip to the Galapagos."[4]

John Dos Passos had a strong influence on *To Have and Have Not.* Dos Passos had been a friend of Hemingway's since 1918, yet there always was a competitive rivalry between the two. In a 1932 letter to Dos Passos, the health of the friendship is evident as Hemingway mixed a response to *1919* with fishing news:

> For Christ sake don't try to do good. Keep on showing it as it is. If you can show it as it really is you will do good. If you try to do good you'll not do any good nor will you show it. That's where the book is so swell because you get so many shots at it through the camera eye—the news reel—the portraits—but because you have those shots don't take it easy in the straight narrative. Write them as though you didn't have any other chance—don't coast along. . . . Everybody well here. We shot 15 foot sawfish—caught 49lb. King—gulf full of sail-

fish. I wish we could live at Tortugas. Remember to get the weather
in your god damned book—weather is very important. (*Selected Letters* 355)

The letter is also interesting as more evidence of Hemingway's formu-
lation of naturalism, and how important environmental factors are to
establishing a scene.[5] In 1934, Dos Passos would join Hemingway in
Havana after recently returning from Hollywood, where he had made a
good deal of money working as the scriptwriter for a Marlene Dietrich
film, *The Devil Is a Woman*. Hemingway would later say, "Poor Dos
got rich out there," and the constant insinuations that Dos Passos had
compromised his integrity began to destroy the long friendship (Baker,
Life 266).[6] By 1936, writes Reynolds, "deeply unhappy with his writing career, angry with critics, and under pressure to produce a successful novel to redeem himself, Hemingway was not made less bitter by
Dos Passos spending his time in Havana correcting galleys for his new
novel, *The Big Money*" (*1930s* 228). The publication of the novel would
allow Dos Passos to beat Hemingway to the honor of appearing on the
cover of *Time*.[7] In the fall and winter of 1936, after quarrelling with Dos
Passos, Hemingway wrote the final book of *To Have and Have Not*.[8]

In a move that would conclusively end their nineteen-year friendship, Hemingway satirized Dos Passos through the character Richard
Gordon and mocked his writing style—"the camera eye"—in chapter
22. The long, precise rendering of Key West street life was Hemingway's
only published description of the city he lived in from 1928 to 1939:

> [Richard Gordon] did not take the bicycle but walked down the
> street. The moon was up now and the trees were dark against it, and
> he passed the frame houses with their narrow yards, light coming
> from the shuttered windows; the unpaved alleys, with their double
> rows of houses; Conch town, where all was starched, well shuttered,
> virtue, failure, grits and boiled grunts, under-nourishment, prejudice,
> righteousness, interbreeding and the comforts of religion; the open-
> doored, lighted Cuban bolito houses, shacks whose only romance
> was their names.

The absence of romance inside these shacks serves to emphasize the different philosophical perspectives of Hemingway and Dos Passos; in this
satire, the former, who considers himself hard boiled and unsentimental,

mocks the latter: Dos Passos is a sap, romanticizing the squalor of the
scene. Hemingway continues:

> The Red House, Chincha's; the pressed stone church; its steeples
> sharp, ugly triangles against the moonlight; the big grounds and the
> long, black domed bulk of the convent, handsome in the moonlight; a
> filling station and a sandwich place, bright-lighted beside a vacant lot
> where a miniature golf course had been taken out; past the brightly
> lit main street with the three drug stores, the music store, the five
> Jew stores, three poolrooms, two barbershops, five beer joints, three
> ice cream parlors, the five poor and the one good restaurant, two
> magazine and paper places, four second-hand joints (one which made
> keys), a photographer's, an office building with four dentists' offices
> upstairs, the big dime store, a hotel on the corner with taxis opposite;
> and across, behind the hotel, to the street that led to jungle town, the
> big unpainted frame house with lights and the girls in the doorway,
> the mechanical piano going, and a sailor sitting in the street; and then
> on back, past the back of the brick courthouse with its clock lumi-
> nous at half-past ten, past the whitewashed jail building shining in
> the moonlight, to the embowered entrance of the Lilac Time where
> motor cars filled the alley. (193–94)

The anger in this satire reveals how much Hemingway has changed
since he began the novel in 1933. The passage reveals a paranoid, jeal-
ous novelist isolated from the intellectual life of cities and cut off from
friends and equals, trying to raise his own status by diminishing the
achievements of another.

No longer elated to be writing a novel with "plenty of action,"
Hemingway is trying to recover his critical reputation, which has been
damaged by *Green Hills of Africa, Death in the Afternoon,* and his ap-
pearances in *Esquire.* In a decade dominated by proletarian literature
and Marxist criticism, Hemingway had, according to many, been conspicuously absent from the battle of the classes.[9] Yet *To Have and Have
Not* is laced with the language of brotherhood, and Hemingway uses the
term to declare a sympathetic bond between those caught in a battle
against natural forces. While the wealthy are asleep in the Key West
harbor, the working class is drinking and fighting in the town's bars.
Cuckolded and abandoned by his wife, the drunken Gordon tries to
fight his wife's lover, Professor MacWalsey. Yet the working-class pa-

trons defend MacWalsey and beat Gordon unconscious. Gordon refuses a taxi ride from MacWalsey and stumbles home. Hemingway writes: "'You can't get him in [the taxi] without fighting him,' the taxi driver said. 'Let him go. He's fine. Is he your brother?' 'In a way,' said Professor MacWalsey" (221). Although they are rivals for the affection of Gordon's wife, as the two intellectual characters in the novel, the two men share a bond, just as the rum-running Morgan and Captain Willie shared a bond in book 2, when Willie says: "Most everybody goes in boats calls each other brother" (83). Indeed, even the reader is addressed as "brother" by Morgan when he narrates: "Brother, don't let anybody tell you there isn't plenty of water between Havana and Key West" (42). The technique allies the reader with the struggling characters of the larger battle of the have-nots against the haves.

In the final pages of the novel, Hemingway returns again to the imagery of the Gulf Stream in an attempt to create some structural unity within a work that he had begun in 1933. Concluding the novel through the eyes of Harry Morgan's working-class widow, Marie, Hemingway writes:

> Through the window you could see the sea looking hard and new and blue in the winter light. A large white yacht was coming into the harbor and seven miles out on the horizon you could see a tanker, small and neat in profile against the blue sea, hugging the reef as she made to the westward to keep from wasting fuel against the stream. (232)

The final paragraph seems tired and workmanlike; this is Hemingway writing when he is tired and uninspired. Yet in the pared-down description of the sea as "hard and new and blue," Hemingway is moving toward the style he would employ in *The Old Man and the Sea*. The Gulf Stream again represents a hard, unforgiving, and timeless natural force that should not be resisted, and Hemingway offers little hope to the struggling working class. The seascape, like a Western landscape, "challenges the body to endure hardship" (Tompkins 71), and the fertility and abundance that characterized the Gulf Stream in book 1 are absent. At the conclusion of the novel, only a grim lesson is harvested; the marlin of book 1 has gotten away.

Book 3 contains some of the most vulgar writing of Hemingway's career, and it is difficult to reconcile those 150 pages with the delicate craftsmanship displayed in *In Our Time* (1925) and *A Farewell to Arms* (1929). The subtleties of characterization and description have been abandoned. Rather than writing as Cézanne painted, Hemingway is writing in the language of comic strips. According to Bert Bender,

> There can be no doubt that Hemingway's chief point about Harry Morgan is his raw, animal vitality; nor should we doubt that this point was calculated, in Hemingway's characteristically combative manner, to irritate readers like Bernard De Voto or T. S. Eliot. (177)

Hemingway was establishing credentials that would allow him to become a member of a more select literary club with William Faulkner, James Jones, and Norman Mailer: the "savage realists." David Shi writes:

> "Savage realists" employed in this fiction the basic elements usually associated with the naturalist impulse: unwholesome social environ-ments and lower-class characters, animal images, event-intoxicated prose written in the superlative degree, an amoral and mechanistic universe seemingly beyond human control or understanding, a wel-ter of violence, capricious instincts, uninhibited lust, and wholesale bloodshed. Characters in their fiction are neither inherently good nor free agents; several lack self-forging initiative and degenerate rather than develop over the course of the novel. (222)

The aggressive masculinity of Harry Morgan has its roots in the doc-trine of the strenuous life, a world that rebels against the effeminate realism of Henry James and William Dean Howells.[10] According to Carlos Baker, Morgan's individualism, his cold courage, his resourceful-ness, and his self-reliance reflect a deeper strain of an "American type" (*Hemingway: The Writer As Artist* 210). This strain of hypermasculin-ity attributed to Morgan was, by extension, attributed to Hemingway and became part of his public image as an American Byron.[11]

Unsurprisingly, Hemingway's major critics have interpreted *To Have and Have Not* as a strain of naturalism. Philip Young, author of *Ernest Hemingway: A Reconsideration*, writes:

> Hemingway's novel is concerned chiefly with the character and experiences of Harry Morgan, and it comes as something of a sur-prise to realize that this "typical Hemingway figure," as he has been called, is actually a rather stock figure in one branch of the tradi-

tional literature of American naturalism. The book is fully enrolled in the primitive school which was founded by Frank Norris and Jack London. Norris's *Moran of the Lady Letty* (1898) is a ludicrous performance, but it introduced to American literature a good deal that would stimulate others, if only to other inferior novels. The book is built around the Have and Have not contrast (and the rich are effete, the poor robust); there is brutality for the subject race, the Chinese, and a lot of deep-sea fishing. . . . Jack London's *Sea Wolf* (1900) came without a blush straight from Moran, but introduced Hemingway's Harry Morgan in a character called Wolf Larson—a virile, brutal individualist whose survival-of-the-fittest ethics are, like Harry's, the interest of the plot. Like Norris's and like Hemingway's, the novel is a sea story charged with cruelty and violence, and the moral—though Larson himself dies alone before he learns it—is that it will not work: no matter how potent and pitiless, a man has no chance alone. (199)

In high school Hemingway had read *The Call of the Wild*, and in later life he would own a copy of London's *Tales of Adventure*, but there is no evidence that he ever read Norris.[12] Hemingway's affinity with this form of naturalism seems to epitomize the cultural moment more than it appears to be a deliberate attempt by Hemingway to become aligned with other writers. Young's ungenerous assessment continues:

Hemingway's book is in the main line of one of our minor literary traditions, in which naturalism goes primitive with a Nietzchean morality in Norris, is tested and found wanting by London. Hemingway simply brought all of this into the line of his development, and redid it for himself with the settings, characters, meanings, and wild brutalities of the prototypes. He also did it better. His novel is a weak one, for him, but nothing makes it look so good as to place it in the company of its progenitors. (199–200)

Although his final phrase offers slight redemption for Hemingway, Young is correct to note that one of Hemingway's methods was to redo things for himself. Carlos Baker wrote:

To Have and Have Not was "about something" Hemingway knew. By the time of the book's publication, he had been living in Key West for nearly ten years, and by 1935 his stucco house on Whitehead Street was listed in the town's guide-book as one of the points of local inter-est for visiting tourists. (*Hemingway: The Writer As Artist* 207)

Hemingway, in this novel, was creating a "knowable community." As Christophe Den Tandt writes,

> Rather than encompassing a boundless field of experience, the real-ist gaze explores what Amy Kaplan, borrowing from Raymond Wil-liams's term, calls "knowable communities"—the family, the work-place, the neighborhood, for instance. Naturalist discourse, on the contrary, relies on documentary discourse to a considerable extent, but it is also obsessed with areas beyond the periphery of positivistic discourse. As such, naturalist discourse addresses the totality of its world, whether to attempt to capture it within its fiction, or to reveal the impossibility of the task. (17)

Although he was always working off other sources, in this instance, Hemingway's source material was first and foremost his own life; but he also drew on his fishing logs, and the lives of his lasting and former friends, creating his own hybrid of naturalism. The foundation of this hybrid resided within Hemingway's observations and judgments. He decided which facts to include in his fiction, and in that way, his natu-ralism was truthful for him.

Baker is another of Hemingway's major interpreters, and he has a more perceptive reading of the novel. Addressing the novel's sympathy for the proletariat, Hemingway's eventual biographer wrote:

> A major difference between this novel and much depression inspired proletarian fiction was that it really embodied the diagnostic notes on decay; it did not preach them. This was a treatise in economics and revolutionary politics which chose to present its findings, not in propagandistic set speeches or in interminable discussions between a young organizer and his experienced mentor, but in straightforward, illustrative dramatic terms. For this reason, and in spite of its serious flaws, *To Have and Have Not* may be said to stand as a somewhat more persuasive social documentary than a great deal of the soap-bubble proletarian literature which appeared, shone brightly, and vanished down wind—through inherent structural weaknesses. an

internal content that was mostly air, and the pressure of changing circumstances—during the period when so many blew the Marxist pipe. (*Hemingway: The Writer As Artist* 206)

Indeed, "straightforward, illustrative dramatic terms" summarizes Hemingway's own form of naturalism, in which he tried to create a portrait of the working class without overlaying it with a socialist gloss.

The world of the Gulf Stream in *To Have and Have Not* was Hemingway's imagined microcosm of a frontier. If, as Henry Nash Smith asserts, James Fenimore Cooper's Leatherstocking "is by far the most important symbol of the national experience of adventure across the continent," then Morgan's life and death become symbolic within the world of the Gulf Stream (61). Baker, too, connects Morgan's milieu with the frontier. While first stating that "Morgan's dying words on the hopeless situation of 'one man alone' ring the knell of nineteenth-century frontier individualism," Baker goes on to note his frontier lineage:

If American readers in the 1930's could not recognize in Harry Morgan a lineal descendant of the American frontiersman, the man who made his own laws and trusted his own judgements, they were perhaps far gone in group thinking. Both in the Far West and in Key West Hemingway had met men of the frontier temperament, so that he did not lack for contemporary models. (*Hemingway: The Writer As Artist* 210)

Robert Stephens considers the novel within the context of the development of Hemingway's intellectual life, especially when paired with the writing he did for *Esquire*. Stephens writes:

The importance of recognizing the direction of Hemingway's cultural thought is not in finding that such thinking existed but in recognizing that it was Hemingway's thinking. Neither unusual nor extraordinary, it nevertheless provided him with a framework for his actions, decisions, and prejudices. A combination of popularized assumptions from the Pastoralists, Wordsworth, Freud, and Spengler, and of relationships systematically described by Frederick Jackson Turner and Walter Prescott Webb, Hemingway's cultural ideology was not a system, but a *faith. Neither provable nor disprovable, it depended for its authority on its emotional convincingness; and Hemingway, finding it suitable to his background and temperament, believed it valid.* (177–78, emphasis added)

The lack of precision in Hemingway's cultural ideology is a result of the intense diversity of Hemingway's interests; he was interested in far too many complex subjects to push his understanding of any one subject to mastery. Indeed, the absence of overt political commentary in *To Have and Have Not* may also result from the fact that Hemingway never took the time to study the subject thoroughly enough to write about it. Moreover, Hemingway was capable of adhering to two conflicting ideas simultaneously, and that was especially evident in his actions on the Gulf Stream as he became a gentle predator, loving the fish he killed while despising the rich yachtsmen he befriended.

Overall, there are few satisfying moments in the novel. *To Have and Have Not* exists as an example of the blending of three elements of American literature: a frontier ideology, naturalism, and proletarian literature. Hemingway brings to this nexus his experiences living in Key West and fishing the Gulf Stream to create a flawed but notable novel. Jane Tompkins's ideas on the films of the West also apply to Harry Morgan's world. The reader only needs to substitute the phrase "Gulf Stream" for the word "West." Tompkins writes:

This West functions as a symbol of freedom, and of the opportunity for conquest. It seems to offer escape from the conditions of life in modern industrial society: from a mechanized existence, economic dead ends, social entanglements, unhappy personal relations, political injustice. The desire to change places also signals a powerful need for self-transformation. The desert light and the desert space, the creak of saddle leather and the sun beating down, the horses' energy and force—these things promise a translation of the self into something purer and more authentic, more real. (4)

Hemingway had interrupted his work on *To Have and Have Not* to write *Green Hills of Africa* from May to November of 1934, and in April of 1936, he finished "The Snows of Kilimanjaro" and "The Short Happy Life of Francis Macomber," two of his finest short stories.[13] Notably, the main character in "The Snows of Kilimanjaro" is a failed writer named Harry, a name that echoes Harry Morgan's. The former's thoughts seem to project the author's own regrets when Hemingway writes: "What was his talent anyway? It was talent all right but instead of using it, he had traded on it. It was never what he had done, but always what he could do" (45). The unevenness of this novel underscores his own artistic fragmentation throughout the 1930s, a time when bullfighting, safaris, and the Spanish civil war all competed for his attention. And as he wrapped up the novel in the final days of 1936, he met the woman who would be his third wife, Martha Gellhorn. By September of 1937, Hemingway would leave his family in Key West to go to Spain with Gellhorn. He would not publish another novel until 1940. The artistic vicissitudes of *To Have and Have Not* mirror the personal tribulations of the author and his own need for self-transformation.

CHAPTER 5

Illustrating the Iceberg

Winslow Homer and *The Old Man and the Sea*

One of the challenges of Hemingway studies is trying to set the date at which Hemingway began *The Old Man and the Sea*. If the date is placed when Hemingway first encountered the key narrative elements of the story, then the earliest he began the novella was July 14, 1932, when Carlos Gutierrez first told him about a giant marlin eaten by sharks.[1] This story was retold by Hemingway in "On the Blue Water: A Gulf Stream Letter," published in *Esquire* in April 1936.[2] If the date is fixed when Hemingway declared unequivocally his intention to write the story, then it must be placed on February 7, 1939, when he wrote to his editor Max Perkins that he had three long stories to write:

> One about the old commercial fisherman who fought the swordfish all alone in his skiff for 4 days and four nights and the sharks finally eating it after he had it alongside and could not get it into the boat. That's a wonderful story of the Cuban coast. I'm going out with old Carlos [Gutierrez] in his skiff so as to get it all right. Everything he does and everything he thinks in all that long fight with the boat out of sight of all other boats all alone on the sea. It's a great story if I can get it right. One that would make the book. (*Selected Letters* 479)

The final choice, of course, would be to put the date in January 1951, when he was definitely working on the novella, which he would finish in draft form by the end of February. On September 1, 1952, it was published in its entirety by *Life* magazine.

The real purpose of reviewing the story's genealogy is to point out how Hemingway wrote and the transformation his method of writing underwent from 1932 to 1952. If the fifteen years from 1926 to 1941 can be understood as a time of enormous creativity for Hemingway, then the time from 1941 to 1951 stands out as a period of stunning un-productiveness. During what should have been the years of his greatest industry, Hemingway wrote nothing but poorly executed journalism. After he returned from Europe at the end of World War II, Hemingway began the "Land, Sea and Air" book, an urtext that became *Across the River and Into the Trees* (1951), *The Old Man and the Sea* (1952), *Islands in the Stream* (1970), and *The Garden of Eden* (1986). *The Old Man and the Sea* emerged from that manuscript in January 1951 (Burwell 51). Writing to Charles Scribner about the novella in October, Hemingway proclaimed: "This is the prose I have been working for all my life that should read easily and simply and seem short and yet have all the dimensions of the visible world and the world of a man's spirit. It is as good prose as I can write now" (*Selected Letters* 738). Indeed, Hemingway's cumulative education in the Gulf Stream manifests itself in *The Old Man and the Sea*. The period from 1941 to 1951 is one of extended gestation, resulting in the stylistic and thematic transformations that had occurred since *To Have and Have Not* (1937). And exploring the aesthetic and thematic connections between Winslow Homer's paintings and *The Old Man and the Sea* makes the broader changes in Hemingway's understanding of the natural world apparent.

Read against the backdrop of Harry Morgan's violent frontier adventures, the tranquility of Santiago's world seems to have sprung forth from the mind of a different writer. The practical and unadorned language portraying the Gulf Stream as a highway has become lyrical, evoking it as a symbol of organic unity within the universe. The naturalism that inspired the evidentiary quality of *To Have and Have Not* has been transposed into an informed style in which the self-taught Santiago reveals broad dimensions of the planet. The brotherhood of cowboys has disappeared, replaced by Santiago's brotherhood with all the flowing life of the Gulf Stream. And while the floating Morgan's final words were that "A man alone ain't got no bloody fucking chance," the resilient Santiago proclaims that "No man is never alone on the sea." In theme and writing style, Hemingway is portraying the Gulf Stream completely anew.

While *To Have and Have Not* begins with a shootout, *The Old Man and the Sea* begins like a folktale, which on one level it is: "He was an old man who fished alone in a skiff in the Gulf Stream and he had gone eighty-four days now without taking a fish." In that one sentence the core of the story resides: a solitary figure is engaged in a struggle with the natural world. In a dramatic transformation, the Gulf Stream has become a space of harmony as a fisherman moves in silent reverence across the water. For Hemingway, the Stream has always been connected metaphorically with Africa, a land whose natural cycles are still, in his perception, undisturbed. His appreciation of the complexity of the Stream was just growing when he went to Tanganyika for his safari. That trip even included deep-sea fishing on the Indian Ocean.[3] Thus the richness and vitality Hemingway encountered in the natural world of Africa was extended to the Gulf Stream. In contrast to Morgan, a character without an inner life, Hemingway dramatizes Santiago's dreams in the opening pages:

> He was asleep in a short time and he dreamed of Africa when he was a boy and the long and the white beaches, so white they hurt your eyes and the high capes and the great brown mountains. He lived along that coast now every night and in his dreams he heard the surf roar and saw the native boats come riding through it. He smelled the tar and oakum of the deck as he slept and he smelled the smell of Africa that the land breeze brought at morning. . . . He no longer dreamed of storms, nor of women, nor of great occurrences, nor of great fish, nor fights, nor contests of strength, nor his wife. He only dreamed of places now and the lions on the beach. (24–25)

Whereas the raw appetites of Morgan were fed by violence, drink, and action, the aging Santiago identifies intimately with the young lions and their vitality. He is a reflective character. As he finds his own strength and passions diminished by time, the lions remind him of the energy that he once possessed, which he now hopes to recapture by catching a fish.

The differences in Hemingway's worldview extend to his informed portrayal of the Gulf Stream. He establishes the sacred tranquility of the milieu in his opening description:

> Sometimes someone would speak in a boat. But most of the boats were silent except for the dip of the oars. They spread apart after they were out of the mouth of the harbour and each one headed for the part of the ocean where he hoped to find fish. The old man knew he was going

far out and he left the smell of the land behind and rowed out into the clean early morning smell of the ocean. He saw the phosphorescence of the Gulf weed in the water as he rowed over the part of the ocean that the fisherman called the great well because there was a sudden deep of seven hundred fathoms where all sorts of fish congregated because of the swirl the current made against the steep walls of the floor of the ocean. Here were concentrations of shrimp and bait fish and sometimes schools of squid in the deepest holes and these rose close to the surface at night where all the wandering fish fed on them. (28–29)

The intense observation inscribed into the fishing logs is now manifesting itself in Hemingway's fiction; details such as the "phosphorescence of the Gulf weed," the contrasting smells, and the precise locations of shrimp, bait fish, and squid reveal a world that was nonexistent for the raw character of Harry Morgan. Hemingway is now a different writer, and Santiago is a new character. He frames a world that will stretch from seven hundred fathoms deep to the heights of Rigel.

In order to create a richer portrayal of the Gulf Stream, Hemingway expanded his portrayal of the senses. He would highlight the element of smells in the novella, as well as enhancing the role of sounds. The scene establishing the setting continues, as Hemingway writes:

In the dark the old man could feel the morning coming and as he rowed he heard the trembling sound of flying fish as they left the water and the hissing that their stiff set wings made as they soared away in the darkness. He was very fond of flying fish as they were his principal friends on the ocean. He was sorry for the birds, especially the small delicate dark terns that were always flying and looking and almost never finding, and he thought, the birds have a harder life than we do except for the robber birds and the heavy strong ones. Why did they make birds so delicate and fine as those sea swallows when the ocean can be so cruel? She is kind and very beautiful. But she can be so cruel and it comes so suddenly and such birds that fly, dipping and hunting, with their small sad voices are made too delicately for the sea. (29)

The universe of birds is outlined from the flying fish, terns, and sea swallows to the robber birds, creating a background that foreshadows Santiago's struggles. Finally, the Gulf Stream, the element that establishes the interconnectedness of all living things, is set forth in its complexity:

He always thought of the sea as la mar which is what people call her in Spanish when they love her. Sometimes those who love her say bad things of her but they are always said as though she were a woman. Some of the younger fishermen, those who used buoys as floats for their lines and had motorboats, bought when the shark livers had brought much money, spoke of her as el mar which is masculine. They spoke of her as a contestant or a place or even an enemy. But the old man always thought of her as feminine and as something that gave or withheld great favours, and if she did wild or wicked things it was because she should not help them. The moon affects her as it does a woman, he thought. (29)

Santiago's language of love, of fickleness, is at odds with the deterministic universe of Morgan. For Hemingway in the 1930s, the harsh laws of nature prevailed, regardless of the acts of man. There is no relationship between man and nature. Yet for Santiago, kinship and flirting with the Gulf Stream are a result of his deep knowledge of its complexity.

If Morgan is a man of action, Santiago is first and foremost an observer. He savors the details he beholds as he tries to live through his eyes. Hemingway writes:

The clouds over the land now rose like mountains and the coast was only a long green line with the gray blue hills behind it. The water was a dark blue now, so dark it was almost purple. As he looked down into it he saw the red sifting of the plankton in the dark water and the strange light the sun made now. He watched his lines to see them go straight down out of sight into the water and he was happy to see so much plankton because it meant fish. The strange light the sun made in the water, now that the sun was higher, meant good weather and so did the shape of the clouds over the land. (35)

As an interpreter of the natural world, Santiago savors the subtle shifts in color he notices, and the plankton and the clouds are elements of nature that he can interpret and act on. The plankton and the good weather are not random facts, but signs of the connections within an ordered natural world.

In *To Have and Have Not*, the enemies Morgan encountered were all men, and the men came in various forms: the rich, the ignorant, and the politically motivated. Santiago's enemies exist within nature, yet nature also has its own scales of justice that sustain balance and order in a delicate world. Although sharks are his most serious enemy, Santiago also worries about Portuguese men-of-war.

> But the bird was almost out of sight now and nothing showed on the surface of the water but some patches of yellow, sun-bleached Sargasso weed and the purple, formalized, iridescent, gelatinous bladder of a Portuguese man-of-war floating close beside the boat. It turned on its side and then righted itself. It floated cheerfully as a bubble with its long deadly purple filaments trailing a yard behind it in the water. "Agua mala," the man said. "You whore." From where he swung lightly against his oars he looked down into the water and saw the tiny fish that were coloured like trailing filaments and swam between them and under the small shade the bubble made as it drifted. They were immune to its poison. But men were not and when some of the filaments would catch on a line and rest there slimy and purple while the old man was working a fish, he would have welts and sores on his arms and hands of the sort that poison ivy or poison oak can give. But these poisonings from the agua mala came quickly and struck like a whiplash. (35–36)

The falseness of the Portuguese man-of-war is one of the ironies of the Gulf Stream that is corrected by another natural element, the turtle. The passage continues:

> The iridescent bubbles were beautiful. But they were the falsest thing in the sea and the old man loved to see the big sea turtles eating them. The turtles saw them, approached them from the front, then shut their eyes so they were completely carapaced and ate them filaments and all. The old man loved to see the turtles eat them and he loved to walk on them on the beach after a storm and hear them pop when he stepped on them with the horny soles of his feet. (36)

The satisfaction that Santiago takes from his revenge is clear, and it implicates him further in the ordered world of the Gulf Stream.

Hemingway continues to create Santiago's world as he describes a "communion" with the marine life of the Stream. Santiago's communions exist in his sacramental relationship with turtles and sharks. Santiago's love for the turtles is synonymous with reverence; if he pays tribute to them, he will receive blessings in return. Hemingway writes:

> He loved green turtles and hawk-bills with their elegance and speed and their great value and he had a friendly contempt for the huge, stupid loggerheads, yellow in their armour-plating, strange in their love-making, and happily eating the Portuguese men-of-war with their eyes shut. He had no mysticism about turtles although he had gone in turtle boats for many years. He was sorry for them all, even the great trunk backs that were as long as the skiff and weighed a ton. Most people are heartless about turtles because a turtle's heart will beat for hours after he has been cut up and butchered. But the old man thought, I have such a heart too and my feet and hearts are like theirs. He ate the white eggs to give himself strength. He ate them all through May to be strong in September and October for the truly big fish. He also drank a cup of shark liver oil each day from the big drum in the shack where many of the fishermen kept their gear. It was there for all fishermen who wanted it. Most fishermen hated the taste. But it was no worse than getting up at the hours that they rose and it was very good against all colds and grippes and it was good for the eyes. (36–37)

Santiago, too, has the heart of a turtle, which will beat long after his death. Santiago, like the turtles, resists death; by consuming the essence of the Stream he will endure and become one with it. Drinking the foul-tasting oil of the hateful sharks is, to Santiago, a duty that reflects his dedication to his vocation as a fisherman, and as an observer, he wants to fortify his eyes. Moreover, the Stream sustains Santiago by providing him nourishment in his battle with the marlin and the sharks. Hemingway writes:

> So he hooked a patch of yellow Gulf weed with the gaff as they passed and shook it so that the small shrimps that were in it fell onto the planking of the skiff. There were more than a dozen of them and they jumped and kicked like sand fleas. The old man pinched their heads off with his thumb and forefinger and ate them chewing up the shells and tails. They were tiny but he knew they were nourishing and they tasted good. (98)

Again, Santiago uses his accumulated knowledge to take advantage of all the Stream offers, and the sacrificial shrimp taste good, unlike the oil of the shark. And when Santiago's hands begin to bleed, he dips them in the sacramental healing water of the Stream:

> Now he knew there was the fish and his hands and back were no dream. The hands cure quickly, he thought. I bled them clean and the salt water will heal them. The dark water of the *true* Gulf is the greatest healer that there is. (99, emphasis added)

The mystical qualities that Hemingway bestows on the Gulf Stream were absent from the straightforward descriptions of *To Have and Have Not.* Harry Morgan and Santiago have distinctly different relationships with the sea. Hemingway had to live with the Stream day after day, writing his observations carefully in the logs, so that once he knew intimately its dimensions, he could write about it fully to construct Santiago's world.

More so than any other form of life in the Stream, the marlin represents a spiritual equal to Santiago, a brother and a partner. Santiago is a widower still mourning his wife's passing, and the devotion between mated marlin echoes his own devotion. In *To Have and Have Not,* when Morgan dies, his wife screams and cries to mourn his death. Santiago's mourning is not public but manifests itself in the observations he makes on the Gulf Stream. Marlin are loyal to their mates, and Santiago reflects on the time he hooked a female marlin, and the male remains devotedly at her side as she is pulled into the boat: "He was beautiful, the old man remembered, and he had stayed" (49–50). The fact that the marlin "stayed" by his mate's side, enduring her death, is model behavior for Santiago, as his own perseverance in the face of this trial is strengthened by his memory of his wife. Thus, whereas Marie Morgan is shown mourning in isolation on a dark dock in Key West, Santiago handles his grief by turning to the Gulf Stream for sustenance and models of endurance.

Although Santiago's solitude in the midst of his battle with the marlin informs it with an epic dimension, he is never self-pitying in his isolation. In contrast to Morgan's famous last line, Hemingway, now working fifteen years later, finds that a man alone does indeed have a chance:

> He looked across the sea and knew how alone he was now. But he could see the prisms in the deep dark water and the line stretching

ahead and the strange undulation of the calm. The clouds were build-
ing up now for the trade wind and he looked ahead and saw a flight of
wild ducks etching themselves against the sky over the water, then
blurring, then etching again and he knew no man was ever alone on
the sea. (61)

Drawing on his sustaining role in the organic unity of the Gulf Stream,
Santiago's isolation is diminished. In the literary naturalism of *To Have
and Have Not*, Hemingway was using an evidentiary eye in his descriptions of Key West, Havana, and the Gulf Stream: he was giving the evidence based on his observation unadorned by any sentiment or judgment.
It is important to note here that Santiago's isolation is assuaged by what
he observes—the "flight of wild ducks etching themselves against the
sky over the water, the blurring, then etching again"—and his knowledge of what that means. Observation, living through one's eyes, is the
path to redemption. Yet one must have essential knowledge, to have
studied the Gulf Stream, in order to interpret fully the observation.

His fight with the marlin takes him beyond observation into a deeper
participation and further communion with the Gulf Stream. The marlin of *To Have and Have Not* were trophies and resources. They had
value as a testament to a man's skill, and value in their worth in the
fish market. In the unified world of Santiago's Stream, however, the
relationship with his prey is intimate. Santiago states: "I love and respect you very much. But I will kill you dead before this day ends" (54).
Santiago's vocation as a fisherman gives him a role in the natural order
of the Gulf Stream that accommodates the marlin's death. Hemingway
writes: "You did not kill the fish only to keep alive and to sell food, he
thought. You killed him for pride and because you are a fisherman. You
loved him when he was alive and you loved him after" (105).

Unlike Morgan, a man without religion, closed off to transformation,
the wiser Santiago is still enhancing his humanity. The marlin has the
power to change him. Once Santiago surrenders the value of victory, it
becomes possible for him to triumph. Hemingway writes: "You are killing me, fish, the old man thought. But you have a right to. Never have
I seen a greater, or more beautiful, or a calmer or more noble thing than
you, brother. Come on and kill me. I do not care who kills who" (92).
The marlin has the power to give something over to him once Santiago
puts all he has against the fish. The battle continues:

He took all his pain and what was left of his strength and his long gone pride and he put it against the fish's agony and the fish came over onto his side and swam gently on his side, his bill almost touching the planking on the skiff and started to pass the boat, long deep, wide, silver and barred with purple and interminable in the water. (93)

Through its death, the marlin becomes unified with Santiago, as Hemingway writes: "When the fish had been hit it was as though he himself were hit" (102). This union between man and fish generates within Santiago the only thing of value he will take from his experience, a lesson, as Santiago's words stand juxtaposed against Morgan's: "A man can be destroyed but not defeated" (103).

The unity that Santiago achieves contrasts with the brotherhood that Morgan sought. In the 1930s, Hemingway created a world in which a brotherhood of working men was an ideal that could be defeated by the rich, by politics, by an indifferent universe. The proletarian ideal displayed by Morgan had limitations, of which, by 1952, Hemingway was acutely aware. Santiago's brotherhood, in contrast, exists within the world of the Gulf Stream, within his deep connection to the lives it sustains. Hemingway writes:

It was dark now as it becomes dark quickly in September. He lay against the worn wood of the bow and rested all that he could. The first stars were out. He did not know the name of Rigel but he saw it and knew soon they would all be out and he would have all his distant friends. "The fish is my friend too," he said aloud. I have never seen or heard of such a fish. But I must kill him. I am glad we do not have to try to kill the stars. . . . I do not understand these things, he thought. But it is good that we do not have to try to kill the sun or the moon or the stars. It is enough to live on the sea and kill our true brothers. (75)

Santiago's solace comes from his understanding of his role with the larger unity of the Gulf Stream, a world that extends to the sun, moon, and stars. Within that sphere, the death of the marlin is clearly the death of an equal. As Santiago says, "I have killed this fish which is my brother" (95).

As a figure at peace with his role in the natural order, Santiago's autodidacticism leads to an informed narrative style. Santiago's world is not merely the world that is seen, but the world he cannot see but knows exists. Morgan's narrative voice was a lens for the reader to view the observed world, not the informed world. Now that the mature Hemingway has studied and lived with the Gulf Stream, he can create a character who sees above and below the surface of the water. Hemingway writes:

> He could not see the green of the shore now but only the tops of the blue hills that showed white as though they were snow-capped and the clouds that looked like high snow mountains above them. The sea was very dark and the light made prisms in the water. The myriad flecks of the plankton were annulled now by the high sun and it was only the great deep prisms in the blue water that the old man saw now with his lines going straight down into the water that was a mile deep. (40)

Even though he cannot observe it, Santiago knows the shore is green, he knows the plankton is there, and he knows the Gulf Stream is a mile deep. The style of the paragraph is reminiscent of the opening paragraph of *A Farewell to Arms* in its use of repetition. The three images of white hang above the "very dark" sea. Yet Santiago is also aware of the high sun, the great blue prisms of the water, and the depth of the Stream. His is an informed vision; he knows what exists below the sea, below the visible part of the iceberg. Appropriately, Hemingway returns to the image of Africa in his final paragraph: "Up the road, in his shack, the old man was sleeping again. He was still sleeping on his face and the boy was sitting by him watching him. The old man was dreaming about the lions" (127). Metaphorically, the Gulf Stream is no longer a frontier; it is an extension of a unified, ordered natural world. Having spent twenty years studying it, Hemingway now has the knowledge that connects him fully with all the dimensions of the Gulf Stream.

Thus, after 1928, Hemingway's vocabulary of writing shifted. He no longer pronounced that he wanted "to write like Cezanne painted." Indeed, up until that time, the Cézanne comments were always private remarks made in letters and unpublished sections of manuscripts.[4] With the publication of *Death in the Afternoon* in 1932, the public Hemingway emerged. Hemingway, the personality, the authority on the subject at hand, became a character in his texts. To be an authority, knowledgeable, it was essential that one have hard-earned knowledge gained from firsthand experience. In *Death in the Afternoon*, Hemingway wrote:

A good writer should know as near everything as possible. Naturally he will not. A great enough writer seems to be born with knowledge. But he really is not; he has only been born with the ability to learn in a quicker ratio to the passage of time than other men and without conscious application, and with an intelligence to accept or reject what is already presented as knowledge. There are some things that cannot be learned quickly, and time, which is all we have, must be paid heavily for in their acquiring. They are the very simplest things and because it takes a man's life to know them the little new that each man gets from life is very costly and the only heritage he has to leave. (191)

With this statement, Hemingway is making his shift away from Cézanne and the uninformed abstraction that his painting represented to him. When he was writing like Cézanne, Hemingway was using colors and repetition to create a canvas for the reader. In the early 1930s, as he is spending more time learning about the Gulf Stream, Hemingway is aware of his own ignorance. Knowledge has become more important to his writing method than effect. The passage in *Death in the Afternoon* continues:

If a writer of prose knows enough about what he is writing about he may omit things that he knows and the reader, if the writer is writing truly enough, will have a feeling of those things as strongly as though the writer had stated them. The dignity of the movement of the iceberg is due to only one-eighth of it being above water. A writer who omits things because he does not know them only makes hollow places in his writing. (192)

In *To Have and Have Not*, Hemingway's naturalist method consisted of him putting in what he knew. The Gulf Stream world was observed and recorded in the narrative in unadorned language. Hemingway did not know enough about the Gulf Stream to omit things. Yet as was recorded in his fishing logs, he was aware that he was accumulating knowledge that could be used or submerged later.

After *The Old Man and the Sea* was published, Hemingway's iceberg principle was used to explain the power and popularity of the novella. The reader's participation was essential to the success of the method. In the words of Robert Stephens, "The reader's response was necessary for the sensing of what was submerged seven-eighths might be. The reader had to respond as much as the writer did to the stimuli of observation, but the stimuli for him came from the created world rather than the raw, experiential world" (216–17). In the *Paris Review* interview with George Plimpton, Hemingway elaborated on his principle of the iceberg:

> If it is any use to know it, I always try to write on the principle of the iceberg. There is seven-eights of it underwater for every part that shows. Anything you know you can eliminate and it only strength- ens your iceberg. It is the part that doesn't show. If a writer omits something because he does not know it then there is a hole in the story. *The Old Man and the Sea* could have been over a thousand pages long and had every character in the village in it and all the pro- cesses of how they made their live, were born, educated, bore chil- dren etc. . . . . First I have tried to eliminate everything unnecessary to conveying experience to the reader so that after he or she has read something it will become a part of his or her experience and seem actually to have happened. This is very hard to do, and I've worked at it very hard. . . . Then the ocean is worth writing about as man is. So I was lucky there. I've seen marlin mate and know about that. So I leave that out. I've seen a school (or pod) of more than fifty sperm whales in that same stretch of water and once harpooned one nearly sixty feet in length and lost him. So I left that out. All the stories I know from the fishing village I leave out. But the knowledge is what makes the underwater part of the iceberg. (235–36)

Hemingway's method, in his mind, is distinctly different from that of writers who have a "phony style," such as Thomas Wolfe and John Dos Passos.[5] In a letter to Max Perkins, Hemingway wrote: "Guys who think they are geniuses because they have never learned to say no to a type- writer are a common phenomenon. All you have to do is to get a phony style and you can write any amount of words" (*Selected Letters* 501).

Since he had been studying the Gulf Stream since 1932 and recording his observations in the fishing logs, his articles for *Esquire,* and his es- says for fishing texts, it is possible to find the passages that Hemingway did indeed leave out. The experience with the sperm whales happened on October 10, 1934, and appears in the *Pilar* log. Hemingway then used it in his May 1936 *Esquire* article "There She Breaches! Or Moby Dick Off the Morro."[6] Yet to the more literal reader of *The Old Man and the Sea,* there are questions about the story that are left unanswered. Perhaps there is no need to include "every character in the village," but more straightforward elements such as the shape of Santiago's boat and how he was fishing and moving about are unclear to readers unfamiliar with marlin fishing in the Gulf Stream. After determining it was inessential, Hemingway left out background information that he had worked hard to accumulate. Thus, because the story is told through the character of Santiago, the whole scene is sacrificed. George Reiger provides supplementary information to the scene for the uninitiated:

> Some fisherman have attempted to reach large fish by drifting for them. . . . Probably the most difficult form of drifting is carried on by commercial fishermen who use this method in taking marlin off the north coast of Cuba between the ports of Cabanas and Santa Cruz del Norte. They call their nearly flat-bottomed skiffs cuchuchas. A small sail carries these fifteen or eighteen-foot craft out to the fishing grounds but, once there, the mast is unstepped; the sail unfurled, and—it is up to the oarsman. Three lines are used, the first one known as the avio de mano or hand tackle and this is lowered to a depth of 90 fathoms. The second line is called avio de hondo or depth tackle, goes down 75 fathoms and is made fast to a stout cane pole which is projected from the bow of the skiff. Any activity on the forward line can be seen by watching the pole. The fisherman at the oar loops the medium line around his big toe and the long line is held by the second fisherman who is in the stern. (262)

Santiago repeatedly states that he misses the boy, Manolin. Hemingway never explains explicitly how his presence would have eased things for Santiago, as this information does. It is an element of the iceberg that is submerged. In "Marlin Off Cuba," Hemingway provided background to the scene that explains more fully Santiago's condition.

> The Cuban fishermen—there are as many as seventy boats fishing marlin regularly within a distance of thirty miles each way along the coast from Havana—set out each morning during the season two or three hours before daylight and drift with the current of the Stream eastward. When the northeast trade wind rises about ten o'clock in the summer mornings, they row their skiffs into the wind to keep their lines straight down from the limber sticks from which they are

looped and which by their sudden dipping will show a fish taking the bait. (55)

In the novella, Hemingway does not include such elements as measured time because it would not be part of Santiago's existence. The number of boats and the distance they travel in a day is also unnecessary background that he chooses to exclude; it would distract the reader from the essential, reduced conditions of the narrative that give it power. Another clear example of what Hemingway left out is apparent in the passage when Santiago first hooks the marlin; Hemingway writes: "The boat began to move slowly off toward the north-west. The fish moved steadily and they traveled slowly on the calm water" (45). Again. in "Marlin Off Cuba," Hemingway had already addressed this moment:

> A big black marlin may jump at once if he is hooked in a tender place, but if he is not being caused any particular pain he will move slowly and heavily, almost like a big shark, circling deep or even swimming toward the boat, and you can often bring him close to the boat before he realizes he is being led, or that he is hooked at all. But when he does realize it he heads straight out for the northwest like an underwater speed boat. (62)

Hemingway is not concerned in the novella with what a marlin may do. It may jump if it is in pain; it may move like a speedboat. Rather, he is providing the reader with essential information about what this marlin does, based on his acquired but submerged knowledge of what they may do.

Beginning in 1932, Hemingway was accumulating very specific facts that he would seek to include as part of the visible iceberg. Thus, there were sections of "Marlin Off Cuba" written in late 1934, developed from the initial interview with Carlos Gutierrez on July 14, 1932, that were clearly transformed into passages in The Old Man in the Sea. Hemingway wrote in the log "males always looking for females—pair when find them—male rush boat and refuse to leave when female hooked."[7] In "Marlin Off Cuba," Hemingway expands on his shorthand:

> Marlin when they are paired are very devoted. The fishermen claim the male fish always hangs back until the female fish has taken a bait, but since the male is often only a fraction of the size of the fe-

male this may not be true altruism. I know that we have frequently hooked the female fish of a pair and had the male fish swim around all during the fight, staying close to the female until she was gaffed. I will tell an incident that anyone is at perfect liberty to doubt but which will be couched for by Captain Joe Russell and Norberg Thompson of Key West who were on the "Anita" at the time when we hooked one fish out of a pair of white marlin. The other fish took a bait a few seconds later but was not hooked. The hooked fish was brought promptly to gaff and the unhooked marlin stayed close beside it, refusing a bait that was passed to it. When the hooked fish was gaffed the unhooked fish swam close beside the boat and when the hooked marlin was lifted in over the gunwale, the unhooked fish jumped high in the air close beside the boat as though to look and see where the hooked fish had gone. It then went down. I swear that this is true but you are quite at liberty to disbelieve it. The hooked fish was a female full of roe. (77)

The passage, as it appears in *The Old Man and the Sea*, has already been examined as an example of Santiago's identification with the marlin, but it is intriguing to note how Hemingway transformed the material. In 1932, Hemingway is a novice to the world of the Gulf Stream and he is gathering raw material. By 1934, he has become a marine scientist, an authority on marlin behavior, stating further in his essay that he has no great respect for them since "the black marlin is a stupid fish," and that "the meat of the very big old black fish is almost uneatable" (64). Then, by 1947, when he is composing the novella, Hemingway is a wizened intimate of the Gulf Stream, able to appreciate the marlin as a spiritual equal to Santiago, a brother and a partner.

Santiago, in many ways, is the perfect character through which to illustrate the iceberg principle. He has a religious devotion to the art of observation, but as someone lacking formal education, he relates information without making scientific pronouncements. Hemingway's handling of the issue of weather is an example of his exclusion from the visible part of the iceberg. In "Cuban Fishing," an article written in 1949 for Brian Vesey-Fitzgerald and Francesca LaMonte's *Game Fish of the World*, Hemingway wrote:

A fisherman, with luck, will find good fishing in almost every month of the year. However the hurricane months are August, September,

and October, and when these storms occur the heavy rains flood the
rivers so that the inner edge of the Gulf Stream prevents the pelagic
fish from traveling over their usual fishing grounds or, at least, keeps
them away. The mass of fresh muddy water also pushes the current
of the Gulf Stream out several miles to sea, especially if the current
is weak, and a series of hurricanes can ruin the September and October fishing for large marlin off the coast of Cuba. (156)

Hemingway is trying to be fully informative in his essay, since this is
essential information for his audience to have. At this time, Hemingway was addressing the same issue in the novella:

If there is a hurricane you always see the signs of it in the sky for days
ahead, if you are at sea. They do not see it ashore because they do not
know what to look for, he thought. The land must make a difference
too, in the shape of the clouds. But we have no hurricane coming
now. He looked at the sky and saw white cumulus built like friendly
piles of ice cream and high above were the tin feathers of the cirrus
against the September sky. (61)

Santiago is reading the signs in the atmosphere and making sense of
them for his own purposes. Santiago does not share with the reader all
the facts that he and Hemingway know, such as that heavy rains "flood
the rivers so that the inner edge of the Gulf Stream prevents the pelagic
fish from traveling over their usual fishing grounds or, at least, keeps
them away." As an observer, Santiago is reading the Gulf Stream and
translating his essential findings.

Hemingway's iceberg principle did not require him to be "truthful"
all the time. Truth, or knowledge, was the starting point; it allowed him
to then elaborate and shape his material. The only serious writing that
Hemingway did from 1941 to 1947 was edit and write the introduction
to the anthology *Men at War* (1942).[8] Hemingway wrote: "A writer's
job is to tell the truth. His standard of fidelity to the truth should be
so high that his invention out of his experience should produce a truer
account than anything factual can be. For facts can be observed badly;
but when a good writer is creating something, he has time and scope
to make it of an absolute truth" (*Hemingway on War* xxiv). There are
inaccuracies in *The Old Man and the Sea*. Robert Weeks has objected
to the characterization of Santiago, calling it "superhuman," and also to

the descriptions of the marlin and the sharks, labeling them "preposter-ous natural history" ("Fakery in *The Old Man and the Sea*" 36–37). In "Hemingway's Extended Vision: *The Old Man and the Sea*," Bickford Sylvester replies to Weeks's criticisms:

> Hemingway is working here partly with new artistic means to match his new vision. Formerly, convinced of the absence of a perceptible order in the world, Hemingway made a fetish of presenting objects exactly as they appeared, so that latent meaning could shine through them without distortion. But here, convinced of the principle behind the facts, he can occasionally take poetic license and present objects for any associational value they may have. Mr. Weeks thinks it is merely a lazy error on Hemingway's part, for example, that Rigel, the first star Santiago sees one night, actually appears close to mid-night in the Caribbean. But Rigel, after all, is a first-magnitude star in the constellation of Orion, the hunter. And it is entirely appropri-ate, symbolically to call attention to Santiago's attunement with the stars in this way. Hemingway is in this story at least attempting to pull the world together, rather than reveal its ironic division. Thus, "the way it was" need no longer be his sole guide as an artist. (95)

To Sylvester, because Hemingway is "convinced of the principle behind the facts," he can extend his ideas beyond them and take poetic license in his representations of the Gulf Stream. In other words, because of his thorough knowledge of what is beneath the surface of the water in his iceberg, the visible part of it can be transformed into something that is representational, rather than realistic.

It seems natural, now, to link *The Old Man and the Sea* with Wins-low Homer's canvases. Yet for Hemingway, the connection had to be earned. It was not until 1948 that Hemingway finally declared his artis-tic affinity with Winslow Homer, stating, "If I could write a book that took place in the Bahamas I would like it to be illustrated by Winslow Homer, provided he did no illustrating but simply painted the Bahamas and what he saw there" (Introduction to *A Farewell to Arms* viii–xi). Hemingway values Homer for his realism; he paints what he sees. Like Santiago, Homer is an observer, a man who lives through his eyes. Just as Cézanne had provided Hemingway with a model for a method of writing, so too would Homer. Hemingway's style changed not because he spent hours viewing Homer's paintings; rather, it was transformed by his intimate contact with the Gulf Stream. Homer's work gained Hemingway's admiration because it portrayed with precision the world in which he was immersed, giving him a visual correlative to the work of his imagination. What Homer represented to Hemingway was a form of selective realism, an objectivity that resided in the observed world. Homer's oil painting *The Gulf Stream* (1899) and his watercolors of the Caribbean served as dual exemplars for Hemingway, as thematically he embraced the former, and in method he embraced the latter (figure 9).

Homer and Hemingway are also united in a belief that realism must be earned. Hemingway worked toward realism every day he was on the Gulf Stream as he recorded his observations, as he questioned other fishermen, as he read about the stars, the tides, and the marine life. According to James D. Hart, unlike literary naturalism, realism in literature, "as an attitude, is relative and no chronological point may be indicated as the beginning of realism" (698). In other words, it is a timeless aesthetic, available to everyone. "Hemingway's style," Derek Walcott wrote, "is realism based on an intimate experience of weather, essential observation that achieves authority" ("On Hemingway," *What the Twilight Says* 108).

Although his method of expression was oil paint and watercolors, Homer's style, too, was rooted in observation. Again, the affinities between Hemingway and Homer through realism are meant to be provocative rather than definitive, yet they are united in their reliance on observation. According to Barbara Novak, Homer's work would fall in the category of "conceptual realism—in which the presentation of the object is controlled by a knowledge of its properties that is tactile and intellectual, rather than optical or perceptual" (223). In 1875, Hemingway's literary ancestor, Henry James, wrote:

> Mr. Homer goes in, as the phrase is, for perfect realism, and cares not a jot for such fantastic hairsplitting as the distinction between beauty and ugliness. He is a genuine painter; that is, to see and reproduce what he sees, is his only care. . . . He not only has no imagination, but he contrives to elevate this rather blighting negative into a blooming and honorable positive. He is almost barbarously simple, and to our eye, he is horribly ugly; but there is nevertheless something one likes about him. (Novak 165)

Not only did Homer portray the Gulf Stream in a direct, representative style, but he also deliberately sought to expose the violence, death, and ugliness that other painters chose to ignore. Like Hemingway, Homer believed in creating from his observations. Although his Caribbean watercolors were done while he visited the region during the winter of 1885–86, Homer's oil paintings were composed long after he returned to Maine. *The Gulf Stream* was a work of imagination that evolved from careful studies and rough sketches.

The artists are also united in their creation of pastoral images. In cities, Homer's paintings of the Caribbean and the Gulf Stream were received as images of an untouched, uncontaminated tropical pastoral. As James Thomas Flexner said, *The Gulf Stream* was evidence of the fact that "tragedy could strike even in this tropical Eden" (163). In the words of Homer's biographer, William Howe Downes,

> It is the most elaborately literary of the artist's tropical motives [*sic*]. In this composition . . . we see a stalwart negro sailor afloat on a dismasted derelict, at the mercy of the elements, in the deep blue Caribbean waters. His drifting craft is surrounded by hideous and voracious sharks, waiting impatiently for their prey to fall into their hungry maws. . . . At some distance from the derelict is a waterspout. The tragedy is enhanced in its horror by the strange beauty of the southern sea. (133)

Yet Downes here does not recognize that this scene is not a tragedy; it is the natural world revealing its laws. The image on the canvas is not a "tropical Eden"; the subject of Homer's painting is the mortality of an individual at the mercy of the Stream.

In *The Old Man and the Sea*, Hemingway's esteem for Homer is manifested thematically, as Santiago's world, too, is neither a frontier nor a pastoral. It is a home, a place where he is never alone. Hemingway uses the Gulf Stream as the stage for Santiago's actions, matching him with the isolated sailor in Homer's painting. Homer's sailor is like Santiago, adrift with the Gulf Stream, uncertain of his fate, surrounded by sharks. The narrative impulse that accompanies Homer's image would have appealed to Hemingway. The sailor's fate, while seemingly hopeless, invites speculation. He could have been a fisherman, like Santiago, who ventured too far out into the Gulf Stream. Although they share the experience of isolation, Hemingway writes, "No man was ever alone on the sea" (61). The words of Santiago fulfill the narrative gap that is present in Homer's *The Gulf Stream* and provide a life-affirming interpretation for the picture. Santiago's journey includes a return trip from the extremes of the Gulf Stream. In the labor of that journey, Santiago affirmed the dimensions of his character with the resolution embedded in the phrase "A man can be destroyed but not defeated" (103). Hemingway creates a unified environment blending Santiago into a system of predators and prey. The contradiction of cruelty and reverence toward nature that besets Hemingway in his *Esquire* letters of the 1930s is gone.

In a number of ways, the iceberg principle can be seen as clarifying Hemingway's appreciation of Homer's work. From Homer's stark canvases Hemingway would learn what details to leave out of his descriptive passages. The verbal technique that Hemingway employs in creating the imaginative landscape shares an affinity with the visual language of Homer. In describing a Homer watercolor, John Wilmerding wrote:

> Homer re-creates the sunlight and reflections of the surface of the water through differing intensities of blue applied by changing lengths and widths of his strokes. He has begun with an underlying pencil sketch to establish the essential network or structure of the picture, over which he has laid horizontals and verticals of varying sizes of his overlapping washes of color reveal a full comprehension of the demands of watercolor for selectivity and boldness. A painter can easily go too far in filling in too much, but Homer's sense of major and minor accents and for expressiveness in dry or fluid brushstrokes makes his work technically polished. Subtle, too, is the compositional balance between animate and inanimate. (*Winslow Homer* 155–56)

In the novella, Hemingway strives to unify the elements of the natural world while applying the lessons of Homer, writing:

> He could not see the green of the shore now but only the tops of the blue hills that showed white as though they were snow-capped and the clouds that looked like high snow mountains above them. The sea was very dark and the light made prisms in the water. The myriad flecks of the plankton were annulled now by the high sun and it was only the great deep prisms in the blue water that the old man saw now with his lines going straight down into the water that was a mile deep. (40)

Hemingway's carefully wrought adjectives establish the range of colors—"white," "snow-capped," "green," "very dark," "blue"—in a way that is applying them to a white canvas, creating an effective response in the reader that is similar to the response evoked by a Homer watercolor. Hemingway's sense of "major and minor accents" and compositional balance is established through his descriptive style. The architectural structure is intact. Like Homer's brushstrokes, each word is perfectly positioned in a sequence that is representational, not abstract.

Hemingway's personal metamorphosis reaches its apogee with *The Old Man and the Sea*. In *To Have and Have Not*, Harry Morgan's primitive perceptions are all that matter. Fifteen years later he would try to harmonize his perceptions, "trying to make . . . a picture of the whole world" (*Selected Letters* 397). In the precise observations of the fishing logs, Santiago's world was created: the wind, the colors of the Gulf Stream, the constellations overhead, and the fish. From all those details, Hemingway chose what to leave out of Santiago's created world, as he constructed the visible, and submerged, dimensions of the iceberg.

The transformation that occurred within Hemingway's philosophy and creative work has not been recognized by either Hemingway scholars or literary critics working in the field of American studies, but like the Gulf Stream, it is a fact. In 1929, Hemingway strove for abstraction in his writing, creating his Cézanne-inspired passages of repeating images of rain, dust, wind, and leaves. The natural world is a place of conquest, a proving ground for his American self. Yet once he immerses himself in the "unexploited country" of the Gulf Stream, he undergoes a subtle but important transformation. The fishing logs reveal Hemingway to be a complex, subtle, and evolving writer, a man on whom nothing was lost. By 1952, Hemingway's Gulf Stream is a harmonious ecosystem, interconnected from its deepest fathoms to the heights of Rigel. What is difficult to convey through a selected presentation of passages from the logs is the sensation one has after reading page after page in Hemingway's hand; the reader is overcome by an immediacy, an intimacy more striking than anything in his fiction. The Gulf Stream becomes real, and the fishing logs are artifacts of a usable past. Hemingway drew on the lessons he learned from other American writers of sea fiction—Melville, Cooper, Crane, and Dana—to create his own study, pouring all his knowledge of the Gulf Stream into *The Old Man and the Sea* to arrive at his aesthetic destination, a mirror of Homer's crystalline canvases portraying the blue water of the sea.

APPENDIX A

Chronology

1931

January	Hemingway begins fishing the Gulf Stream, entertaining guests such as Max Perkins, Josie Herbst, and Mike Strater.

1932

April 20	Hemingway leaves for Cuba and his first sustained experience fishing the Gulf Stream. He rents Joe Russell's launch, the *Anita*.
July 14	Hemingway meets Carlos Gutierrez, from whom he gains essential knowledge about the Gulf Stream and marlin. In his initial interview, he hears the story of an old fisherman pulled out to sea by a giant marlin.
May 20	Hemingway returns to Key West.
September 23	*Death in the Afternoon* is published in New York City.

1933

January 25–July 20	Hemingway returns to Cuba with the *Anita* and fishes the Gulf Stream.
February	Hemingway begins "One Trip Across," part 1 of *To Have and Have Not*.
March 13	Hemingway asks Perkins for a letter certifying he is at work on a book about the fish of the Gulf Stream.
July	Hemingway catches a 468-pound, twelve-foot-eight-inch-long marlin, the biggest marlin ever caught off the Cuban coast with rod and line.

July 21– August 3	Hemingway in Key West preparing for his departure to Europe and Africa.

July 21–
August 3   Hemingway in Key West preparing for his departure to Europe and Africa.

August   "Marlin Off the Morro," Hemingway's first contribution to *Esquire*, appears in the premier issue of the magazine.

October   Hemingway departs for his African safari. He completes "One Trip Across" while in Paris.

October 16   Hemingway writes Mrs. Paul Pfeiffer about a story he wrote to "rinse his mouth out," "One Trip Across" (*Selected Letters* 397).

October 27   *Winner Take Nothing*, Hemingway's collection of short stories, is published in New York City.

December 20   African safari begins in Tanganyika.

1934

February 28   Safari ends.

March 3   Hemingway receives a letter from Charles Cadwalader, director of the Academy of Natural Sciences of Philadelphia, asking for his assistance in conducting research in Cuban waters.

April 12   Hemingway returns to Key West. Hemingway writes Max Perkins that he is working on a Gulf Stream book. "One Trip Across" is published in *Cosmopolitan*.

May 11   Hemingway accepts delivery of the *Pilar*, his new fishing boat, and begins working on *Green Hills of Africa*.

July 18   Joined by Arnold Samuelson, Hemingway takes the *Pilar* to Havana, where he is met by Charles Cadwalader and Henry Fowler from the Academy of Natural Sciences.

August   "Out in the Stream: A Cuban Letter" is published in *Esquire*.

October 18   John Dos Passos arrives in Havana to join Hemingway.

October 26   Hemingway and Dos Passos return to Key West.

November 16   Draft of *Green Hills of Africa* is finished.

1935

April 14   Hemingway takes the *Pilar* to Bimini for tuna fishing.

May   First installment of *Green Hills of Africa* is printed in *Scribner's Magazine*.

May 15   *American Big Game Fishing*, edited by Eugene V. Connett, is published, with chapter 2, "Marlin Off Cuba," written by Hemingway.

May 25   Hemingway catches a world-record 381-pound bluefin tuna off Bimini.

June 22	Hemingway catches a 786-pound mako shark, the third-largest ever landed in the world by rod and reel, off the coast of Bimini.
August 15	Hemingway returns from Bimini to Key West.
September 17	"Who Murdered the Vets?" is published in *The New Masses*.
October 25	*Green Hills of Africa* is published.

1936

April	Hemingway finishes "The Snows of Kilimanjaro" and "The Short Happy Life of Francis Macomber." "On the Blue Water: A Gulf Stream Letter," in which the story of a fisherman pulled out to sea by a huge marlin that he eventually loses to sharks is told, is published in *Esquire*.
April 27	Hemingway takes the *Pilar* to Havana for marlin fishing.
May	"There She Breaches! Of Moby Dick Off the Morro" is published in *Esquire*.
June 4	Hemingway leaves for Bimini.
August	"Snows of Kilimanjaro" is published in *Esquire*.
September	"The Short Happy Life of Francis Macomber" is published in *Esquire*.
November 23	The Bahamas Blue Marlin and Tuna Club is founded in Bimini by Hemingway, Michael Lerner, Thomas Shevlin, A. O. H. Baldridge, Julio Sanchez, S. Kip Farrington, and Erl Roman. The club is the precursor of the International Game Fishing Association.
December	Hemingway meets Martha Gellhorn in Key West.

1937

January 2	*To Have and Have Not* is finished.
February 7	Hemingway arrives in Paris and travels to Spain to cover the civil war.
May 12	Hemingway returns to New York.
May 26	Hemingway leaves for Bimini, which will be his base in the midst of trips to New York, the White House, and Hollywood. The additional travel was to raise money for the Loyalist cause in Spain.
August 3	Hemingway returns from Bimini to Key West.
October 15	*To Have and Have Not* is published.
December	*Atlantic Game Fishing* by S. Kip Farrington is published, with an introduction by Hemingway.

1939

February 7   Hemingway writes his editor Max Perkins that one of three long stories he wants to write is about a commercial fisherman fighting a marlin alone for four days.

May   Martha Gellhorn rents the Finca Vigía in Cojimar, Cuba.

June 7   The International Game Fish Association is formally founded. Hemingway will serve as vice president until his death in 1961.

December 19   Hemingway returns from Idaho, finds his Key West home closed up, and joins Gellhorn in Cuba.

1940–44

Except for his time hunting German submarines in the Caribbean from April 1942 to February 1944, Hemingway's activities in these years do not involve the Gulf Stream.

1945

October   Hemingway begins the "Land, Sea and Air" book, the urtext that became *Across the River and Into the Trees*, *The Old Man and the Sea*, *Islands in the Stream*, and *The Garden of Eden* (Burwell 1).

1944–47

Hemingway's activities in these years do not involve the Gulf Stream.

1948

September   Hemingway probably begins writing *Islands in the Stream*.

1949

July   "The Great Blue River" is published in *Holiday*.

November   *Game Fish of the World*, edited by Brian Vesey-Fitzgerald and Francesca LaMonte, is published, with a chapter entitled "Cuban Fishing" by Hemingway.

1950

April   Hemingway begins writing the Cuba section of what will become *Islands in the Stream*.

December   Hemingway completes his Bimini novel, titling it *Islands in the Stream*.

1951

January
: Hemingway works on *The Old Man and the Sea* through the end of February, calling it finished at 26,531 words.

October
: Hemingway writes Charles Scribner about *The Old Man and the Sea*, proclaiming: "This is the prose I have been working for all my life."

1952

September
: *Life* publishes *The Old Man and the Sea* in a single issue, having paid Hemingway $40,000.

Selections from Hemingway's Library

Based on Brasch and Sigman's *Hemingway's Library: A Composite Record*, this appendix lists books that may shed light on the composition of *To Have and Have Not* and *The Old Man and the Sea*. Not included are the books on hunting in Africa, of which there are well over a hundred, or the books on the American West, two topics that also influenced Hemingway's thoughts on the Gulf Stream. Incomplete citations reflects the incomplete citations in Brasch and Sigman. According to Brasch, "Hemingway held every book in his hand."

Alexander, Wilfrid Backhouse. *Birds of the Ocean: A Handbook for Voyagers Containing Descriptions of All the Sea-Birds of the World, with Notes on Their Habits and Guides to Their Identification.* New York: Putnam, 1928.

Arnold, Augusta Foote. *The Sea-Beach at Ebb-Tide: A Guide to the Study of the Seaweeds and the Lower Animal Life Found Between Tidemarks.* New York: Century, 1901.

Audubon, John James. *The Birds of America.* Foreword and descriptive captions by John Vogt. New York: Macmillan, 1946.

Austin, A. B., comp. *An Angler's Anthology.*

Baldwin, Hanson Weightman. *Sea-Fights and Ship Wrecks: True Tales of the Seven Seas.* Garden City, NJ: Hanover, 1955.

———. *What the Citizen Should Know About the Navy.* New York: Norton, 1941.

Bandini, Ralph. *Men, Fish and Tackle: The Story of J. A. Coxe as Told to Ralph Bandini.* Bronson, MI: Bronson Reel, 1936.

Barbour, Thomas. *Naturalist at Large*. Boston: Little, Brown, 1945.

———. *A Naturalist in Cuba*. Boston: Little, Brown, 1945.

———. *That Vanishing Eden: A Naturalist's Florida*. Boston: Little, Brown, 1945.

Barnard, Keppel Harcourt. *A Beginner's Guide to South African Shells*. Cape Town: Miller, 1951.

———. *A Pictorial Guide to South African Fishes, Marine and Freshwater*. Cape Town: Miller, 1947.

Beebe, William, ed. *The Book of Naturalists: An Anthology of the Best Natural History*. New York: Knopf, 1945.

Birds in Natural Colors: A Monthly Serial. Bound edition. Chicago: Mumford, 1899.

Blond, George. *The Great Story of Whales*. Trans. James Cleugh. Garden City, NY: Hanover, 1955.

The Book of Fishes: Game Fishes, Food Fishes, Shellfish and Curious Citizens of American Ocean Shores, Lakes and Rivers. Washington, DC: National Geographic Society, 1924.

Breder, Charles Marcus. *Field Book of Marine Fishes of the Atlantic Coast from Labrado to Texas; Being a Short Description of Their Characteristics and Habits with Keys for Their Identification*.

Burns, Eugene. *The Complete Book of Fresh and Salt Water Spinning*. New York: Barnes, 1955.

Camp. Raymond Russell, ed. *The Fireside Book of Fishing: A Selection from the Great Literature of Angling*. New York: Simon & Schuster, 1959.

Carson, Rachel. *The Sea Around Us*. New York: Oxford University Press, 1951.

Connett, Eugene V., ed. *American Big Game Fishing*. New York: Derrydale, 1935.

Cooper, Eric, ed. *Sea Fishing*. Philadelphia: Lippincott, 1934.

Copley, Hugh. *The Game Fishes of Africa*. London: Witherby, 1952.

———. *Wonders of the Kenya Seashore: A Short Guide to the Birds, Fishes, Shells, and Other Forms of Life Found on the Seashore*. Nairobi: Highway Press, 1946.

Dana, Richard Henry Jr. *To Cuba and Back: A Vacation Voyage*. Boston: Ticknor & Fields, 1859.

———. *Two Years Before the Mast*. London: Dent, 1925.

Darwin, Charles Robert. *Charles Darwin and the Voyage of the Beagle· Unpublished Letters and Notebooks*. Ed. Nora Barlow. New York: Philosophical Library, 1946.

———. *The Darwin Reader*. Ed. Marston Bates and Philip S. Humphrey. New York: Scribners, 1956.

Descartes, René. *Discourse on the Method of Rightly Conducting the Reason and Seeking of Truth in the Sciences.* Trans. John Veitch. LaSalle, IL: Open Court, 1945.

Devoe, Alan. *The Naturalist's Christmas.* New York: n.d.

Dimock, Anthony Weston. *The Book of the Tarpon.* New York: Outing, 1911.

Douglas, Marjory Stoneman. *The Everglades: River of Grass.* New York: Rinehart, 1947.

Dow, George Francis. *Whale Ships and Whaling: A Pictorial History of Whaling During Three Centuries.* Salem, MA: Marine Research Society, 1925.

Farrington, Selwyn Kip. *Atlantic Game Fishing.* Introduction by Ernest Hemingway. New York: Kennedy, 1937.

———. *Atlantic Game Fishing.* Introduction by Ernest Hemingway. New York: Kennedy, 1957.

———. *A Book of Fishes.* Philadelphia: Blakiston, 1946.

———. *Fishing the Pacific.* New York: Coward-McCann, 1942.

Farson, Negley. *Going Fishing.* New York: Harcourt Brace, 1943.

Fisher, James, and R. N. Lockley. *Sea-Birds: An Introduction to the Natural History of the Sea-birds of the North Atlantic.* Boston: Houghton Mifflin, 1954.

Francis, Francis. *A Book on Angling; Being a Complete Treatise on the Art of Angling in Every Branch with Explanatory Plates, etc.* Ed. Sir Herbert Maxwell. London: Jenkins, 1920.

Furtnas, Joseph Chamberlin. *Anatomy of Paradise: Hawaii and the Islands of the South Seas.* New York: Sloane, 1948.

Gessler, Clifford. *Hawaii: Isles of Enchantment.* New York: Appleton-Century, 1938.

Glazier, Willard. *Down the Great River; Embracing an Account of the Discovery of the Source of the Mississippi, Together with Views, Descriptive and Pictorial of the Cities, Towns, Villages, and Scenery on the Banks of the River, as Seen during a Canoe Voyage of Over Three Thousand Miles from Its Head Waters to the Gulf of Mexico.* Philadelphia: Hubbard, 1893.

Greenwood, James. *Wild Sports of the World: A Natural History and Adventure.* London: Ward, Lock & Tyler, 1880.

Gregg, William H. *Where, When and How to Catch Fish on the East Coast of Florida.*

Gregory, William K., and Francesca LaMonte. *The World of Fishes: A Survey of Their Habits, Relationship and History and Guide to the Fish Collections of the American Museum of Natural History.* New York: American Museum of Natural History, 1947.

Grey, Zane. *An American Angler in Australia.* New York: Harper, 1937.

————. *Tales of Swordfish and Tuna.* London: Hodder & Stoughton, 1927.

————. *Tales of Tahitian Waters.* New York: Harper, 1931.

————. *Tales of the Angler's Eldorado: New Zealand.*

Haley, Nelson Cole. *Whale Hunt: The Narrative of the Voyage by Nelson Cole Haley, Harpooner in the Ship Charles W. Morgan, 1849–1853.* New York: Washburn, 1948.

Hardy, Alister Clavering. *The Open Sea: Its Natural History.* Vol. 1: *The World of Plankton.* Vol. 2: *Fish and Fisheries.* Boston: Houghton Mifflin, 1956, 1959.

Hardy's Angler's Guide. London, 1924.

Hatley, T. L., and Hugh Copley. *Angling in East Africa; With Some Account of East African Fish.*

Heyerdahl, Thor. *Kon-Tiki: Across the Pacific by Raft.* Trans. F. H. Lyon. Chicago: Rand McNally, 1950.

Hickey, Joseph. *A Guide to Bird Watching.* London: Oxford University Press, 1943.

Hoffman, Ralph. *Birds of the Pacific States.* Boston: Houghton Mifflin, 1927.

Holder, Charles Frederick. *The Big Game Fishes of the United States.* New York: Macmillan, 1941.

Hornell, James. *Fishing in Many Waters.* Cambridge: University Press, 1908.

Horvath, Odon von. *The Age of the Fish.* Trans. R. Willis Thomas. New York: Dial, 1939.

Hudson, W. H. *Adventures Among Birds.* London: Dent, 1928.

————. *The Book of a Naturalist.*

Hughes, Richard A. W. *In Hazard: A Sea Story.* London: Chatto & Windus, 1938.

————. *A High Wind in Jamaica.* New York: Modern Library, 1929.

————. *The Innocent Voyage.* Introduction by Louis Untermeyer. New York: Limited Editions, 1944.

Hughes-Parry, Jack. *Fishing Fantasy: A Salmon Fisherman's Notebook.* London: Eyre & Spottiswoode, 1949.

The International Game Fish Association. *Organization and Rules.* New York: American Museum of Natural History, 1945.

————. *World Record Marine Game Fishes.* Miami, 1959.

————. *World Record Marine Game Fishes.* Miami, 1960.

————. *Yearbook.* New York: American Museum of Natural History, 1952.

Jennison, George. *Natural History, Animals: An Illustrated Who's Who of the Animal World.* London: Black, 1927.

Jordan, David Starr. *Fishes.* New York: Appleton, 1925.

————. *The Fish Fauna of the California Tertiary.* Stanford, CA: Stanford University, 1921.

Jordan, David Starr, and Carl Leavitt Hubbs. *Studies in Icthylogy: A Monographic Review of the Family of* Atherinidae *or Silversides.* Stanford, CA: Stanford University, 1919.

Kaplan, Moise N. *Big Game Angler's Paradise: A Complete Non-technical Narrative-treatise on Saltwater Gamefishes and Angling in Florida and Elsewhere.* New York: Liveright, 1937.

———. *Big Game Fisherman's Paradise: A Complete Treatise on Angling Philosophy, Sidelights, and Scenes in Florida Saltwater Fishing Ventures.* Tallahassee, FL: Department of Agriculture, 1956.

Knight, John Alden. *Field Book of Fresh Water Angling.* New York: Putnam, 1944.

———. *Modern Fly Casting.* New York: Scribners, 1942.

LaMonte, Francesca Raimonde. *Marine Game Fishes of the World.* Garden City, NY: Doubleday, 1953.

———. *North American Game Fishes.* Garden City, NY: Doubleday, Doran, 1945.

———. *A Review and Revision of the Marlins, Genus* Makiara. New York: American Museum of Natural History, 1955.

LaMonte, Francesca Raimonde, and Donald E. Marcy. *Icthyological Contributions to the International Game Fish Association.* New York, 1941.

Latil, Pierre de, and Jean Rivoire. *Man and the Underwater World.* Trans. Edward Fitzgerald. New York: Putnam, 1956.

Leopold, Aldo. *Game Management.* New York: Scribners, 1933.

Lincoln, Frederick Charles. *The Migration of American Birds.* Illustrated by Louis Aggasiz Fuertes. New York: Doubleday, Doran, 1939.

Ludwig, Emil. *The Mediterranean: Saga of a Sea.* Trans. Barrows Mussey. New York: Whittlesey House, McGraw-Hill, 1942.

Major, Harlan. *Salt Water Fishing Tackle.* New York: Funk & Wagnalls, 1948.

Markman, Harvey C. *Fossils: A Story of the Rocks and Their Record of Prehistoric Life.* Popular Series No. 3. Denver, CO: Denver Museum of Natural History, 1954.

Matthiessen, Peter. *Wildlife in America.* New York: Viking, 1959.

Mitchell-Hedges, Frederick Albert. *Battles with Giant Fish.*

Mitchell-Henry L. *Tunny Fishing at Home and Abroad.* London: Rich & Cowan, 1934.

Monsarrat, Nicholas. *The Cruel Sea.* London: Cassell, 1951.

Morgan, Ann Haven. *Field Book of Ponds and Streams: An Introduction to the Life of Fresh Water.* New York: Putnam, 1930.

Morrill, George. *Dark Sea Running.* New York: McGraw-Hill, 1959.

Morris, Percy A. *A Field Guide to the Shells of Our Atlantic Coast.* Boston: Houghton Mifflin, 1947.

Needham, Paul Robert. *Trout Streams: Conditions That Determine Their Productivity and Suggestions for Stream and Lake Management.* Ithaca, NY: Comstock, 1938.

Norris, Thaddeus. *The American Angler's Book, Embracing the Natural History of Sporting Fish, and the Art of Taking Them, with Instructions in Fly-Fishing, Fly-Making, and Rod-Making, and Directions for Fish Breeding, to Which Is Added* Dies Doscatoriae, *Describing Noted Fishing Places, and the Pleasures of Solitary Fly-Fishing.* Philadelphia: Porter & Coates, 1864.

Norton, Mortimer. *Salt Water Sports Fishing, by Old Ai.* n.p. 1948.

Olcott, William Tyler. *The Book of the Stars for Young People.* New York: Putnam, 1923.

Olcott, William Tyler, and Edmund Putnam. *Field Book of the Skies: A Presentation of the Main Facts of Modern Astronomy and a Practical Field Guide for the Observer.* New York: Putnam, 1929.

Ott, Wolfgang. *Sharks and Little Fish.* Trans. Ralph Manheim. New York: Dell, 1959.

Outwaite, Leonard. *Atlantic Circle: Around the Ocean with Winds and Tides.* New York: Scribners, 1931.

Peterson, Roger Tory. *Birds Over America.* New York: Dodd, Mead, 1948.

———. *Field Guide to the Birds.*

———. *A Field Guide to the Western Birds.* Boston: Houghton Mifflin, 1941.

———. *How to Know the Birds.* New York: New American Library, 1957.

Pettingill, Olin Sewall. *A Guide to Bird Finding East of the Mississippi.* New York: Oxford University Press, 1951.

———. *A Guide to Bird Finding West of the Mississippi.* New York: Oxford University Press, 1953.

Pinchot, Gifford. *Just Fishing Talk.* New York: Telegraph, 1936.

Polowe, David. *Navigation for Mariners and Aviators.* New York: Cornell Maritime, 1942.

Pope, Clifford Hillhouse. *Turtles in the U.S. and Canada.*

Pope, Edith. *River in the Wind.* New York: Scribners, 1954.

Pough, Richard Hooper. *Audubon Bird Guide: Small Land Birds of Eastern and Central North America from Southern Texas to Central Greenland.* Garden City, NY: Doubleday, 1951.

———. *Audubon Water Bird Guide: Water, Game and Large Birds, Eastern and Central North America, from Southern Texas to Central Greenland.* Garden City, NY: Doubleday, 1951.

Radcliffe, William. *Fishing from the Earliest Times.* London: Murray, 1926.

Roberts, Walter Adolphe. *The Caribbean: The Story of Our Sea of Destiny.* Indianapolis: Bobbs-Merrill, 1940.

Roosevelt, Robert Barnwell. *Superior Fishing; or The Striped Bass, Trout, Black-Bass and Blue-Fish of the Northern States.* New York: Orange Judd, 1884.

Roughley, Theodore Cleveland. *Wonders of the Great Barrier Reef.* New York: Scribners, 1947.

Roule, Louis. *Fishes: Their Journeys and Migrations.* Introduction by William Beebe. Trans. Conrad Elphinstone. New York: Norton, 1933.

Sanford, Leonard Cutler, Louis Bennet Bishop, and Theodore Van Dyke. *The Water Fowl Family.* New York: Macmillan, 1924.

Schenck, Hilbert van Nydeck, and Henry Kendall. *Shallow Water Diving and Spearfishing.* Cambridge, MD: Cornell Maritime, 1954.

Schrenkesisen, Raymond Martin, ed. *Fishing for Salmon and Trout.* Garden City, NY: Doubleday, 1937.

Simpson, George Gaylord. *The Rise of Mammals: After Dominating the World for Millions of Years the Dinosaurs Come to an Abrupt End and the Meek Inherit the Earth.* New York: American Museum of Natural History, 1951.

Smith, Frederick George Walton, and Henry Chapin. *The Sun and the Sea, and Tomorrow: Potential Sources of Food, Energy, and Minerals from the Sea.* New York: Scribners, 1954.

Solar, Antonio G. *The Guide to Hunting and Fishing in Cuba; Published to Give Visiting Sportsmen the Knowledge and Experience of the Cubans.* Havana, 1958.

Southard, Charles Zibeon. *The Evolution of Trout and Trout Fishing in America.*

Sparrow, Walter Shaw. *Angling in British Art Through Five Centuries: Prints, Pictures, Books.*

Spectorsky, Auguste C., ed. *The Book of the Sea; Being a Collection of Writings About the Sea in All Its Aspects.* New York: Grosset & Dunlap, 1958.

Streever, Fred. *A New Fishing Technique: Deep Trolling with Fine Wire.* New York, n.d.

Sturgis, Bertha. *Field Book of Birds of the Panama Canal Zone.*

Sues, Ilona Ralf. *Shark's Fins and Millet.* Boston: Little, Brown, 1944.

Tannehill, Ivan Ray. *Hurricanes: Their Nature and History, Particularly Those of the West Indies and the Southern Coasts of the United States.* Princeton, NJ: Princeton University Press, 1938.

Taverner, Eric. *Trout Fishing from All Angles.* London: Seely, 1933.

Teale, Edwin Way. *Adventures in Nature: Selections from the Outdoor Writings of Edwin Way Teale.* New York: Dodd, Mead, 1959.

Teasdale, Sara. *Rivers to the Sea.* New York: Macmillan, 1915.

Tee-Van, John, et al., eds. *Fishes of the Western North Atlantic.* New Haven, CT: Sears Foundation for Marine Research, Yale University, 1948.

Thomas, George Clifford, and George C. Thomas III. *Game Fish of the Pacific, Southern Californian and Mexican.* Philadelphia: Lippincott, 1930.

Tompkins, Warwick Miller. *The Coastwise Navigator.* New York: Dodd, Mead, 1940.

———. *The Offshore Navigator.* New York: Dodd, Mead, 1942.

Tongue, Cornelius [Cecil]. *Records of the Chase and Memoirs of Celebrated Sportsmen, Illustrating Some of the Usages of Olden Times and Comparing Them with Prevailing Customs, Together with an Introduction to Most of the Fashionable Hunting Countries and Comments.* London: Longman, Brown Green & Longmans, 1854.

Towner Coston, Harry Ernest. *Speckled Nomads: A Tale of Trout of Two Rivers.* New York: Macmillan, 1939.

Towner Coston, Harry Ernest, F. T. K. Pentelow, and R. W. Butcher. *River Management: The Making, Care and Development of Salmon and Trout Rivers.* Philadelphia: Lippincott, 1936.

University of Miami, Coral Gables. Institute of Marine Science. *Lou-Marron-University of Miami, Pacific Billfish Expedition: Preliminary Report for 1954.* Coral Gables, FL, 1955.

U.S. Coast Guard and Geodetic Survey. *Inside Route Pilot: Intracoastal Waterway, New York to Key West.* Washington, DC: U.S. Government Printing Office, 1936.

———. *United States Coast Pilot, Atlantic Coast. Section D. Cape Henry to Key West.* Washington, DC: U.S. Government Printing Office, 1928.

———. *United States Coast Pilot, Gulf Coast. Key West to the Rio Grande.* Washington, DC: U.S. Government Printing Office, 1936.

U.S. Hydrographic Office. *Navigation Tables for Sailors and Aviators.* Washington, DC: U.S. Government Printing Office, 1937.

———. *Sailing Directions for the West Indies.* Issued under the authority of the Secretary of the Navy. Washington, DC: U.S. Government Printing Office, 1936.

Verrill, Alpheus Hyatt. *Strange Sea Shells and Their Stories.* Boston: Page, 1936.

Vesey-Fitzgerald, Brian Seymour, and Francesca LaMonte, eds. *Game Fish of the World.* New York: Harper, 1949.

Walton, Issak. *The Compleat Angler; or The Contemplative Man's Recreation of Issak Walton and Charles Cotton.* Boston: Little, Brown, 1922.

Watkins-Pitchford, Denys James [B. B.], comp. *The Fisherman's Bedside Book.* New York: Scribner, 1946.

Williams, Taylor. *Hunting & Fishing.* Idaho, n.d.

Yale, Leroy Milton, et al. *Angling.* New York: Scribners, 1897.

Zim, Herbert Spencer, and Robert H. Baker. *Stars: A Guide to the Constellations, Sun, Moon, Planets and Other Features of the Heavens.* New York: Simon & Schuster, 1951.

Zim, Herbert Spencer, and Lester Ingel. *Seashores: A Guide to Animals and Plants Along the Beaches.* New York: Simon & Schuster, 1955.

Zim, Herbert Spencer, and Hurst H. Shoemaker. *Fishes: A Guide to Fresh and Saltwater Species.* New York: Simon & Schuster, 1956.

Notes

1. The Sea Change Part I

1. Hemingway's library attests to this preoccupation with his place in American literary history, and his bookshelves contained some of the essential reading for a course in American studies. In addition to Cooper, Herman Melville, Stephen Crane, Henry Adams, Van Wyck Brooks, Waldo Frank, H. L. Mencken, F. O. Maittheisen, Jack Kerouac, and Norman Mailer were all represented on the shelves of the Finca Vigia, his home in Cuba (see Brasch and Sigman).

2. Many of the logs have not been thoroughly examined. Michael Reynolds, the Hemingway scholar most familiar with the logs, died of cancer in 2000. There are only three published articles that refer to the logs. See Janice Byrne, Linda Patterson Miller, and William Braasch Watson.

3. In his library, Hemingway had two copies of *Typee* and one copy of *Moby-Dick.* See Brasch and Sigman 249–50.

4. Notable entries will be quoted in part, but to avoid uninteresting language, few entries will be quoted in full. Although I highlight passages in the logs due to their content, my examination of them follows their natural chronology so that Hemingway's transformation from a novice to an expert can be fully appreciated. I have maintained the short length of the lines of the fishing logs in an effort to show the reader how Hemingway actually composed the logs. The line breaks function as a rough form of enjambment, as closely related words fall on different lines. While the majority of the line breaks exist purely for expediency, there are notable exceptions. Any underlining is Hemingway's, and his imperfect spelling, too, is left intact. Unsurprisingly, Hemingway's punctuation is sporadic at best in the logs; he often substituted dashes for periods and ignored capitalization. Italics will be used

to highlight language that may not initially be notable but is ultimately significant. The numbers in parentheses are my own addition and refer to the pages in Hemingway's notebook, which is unnumbered.

5. One arroba equals 25 pounds. Thus, this marlin weighed 1,125 pounds.

6. The debate about the origins of *The Old Man and the Sea* is explored more fully in my article "Hemingway's Hawaiian Honeymoon," 65.

7. The entry of May 20 was the last one for the 1932 fishing season.

8. The number in parentheses was actually circled by Hemingway, as he made a running count of the number of marlin they had caught that season. By this point (obviously), it was thirty-two.

9. The book was published in New York on September 23, 1932. The *New Yorker* called the book "suicidal" on Hemingway's part, and the *New York Times'* review stated: "Action and dialogue are his best weapons. To the degree that he dilutes them with philosophy and exposition he weakens himself" (Reynolds, *1930s* 101–2).

10. Hemingway would never take a public stand on Cuban political issues. From the time he made Cojimar his home in 1939 until his final departure after the Castro revolution had succeeded in July of 1960, Hemingway discreetly kept his opinions unpublished.

11. Michael Reynolds uses the two logs from 1933 as separate entities. One log is referred to in his notes to *Hemingway: The 1930s* as "EH calendar log, 1933"; the other log is referred to as "*Anita* log, 1933." See Reynolds, *1930s* (332) for an example. Because these documents overlap from April 12 to May 15, I consider them here as one organic whole. With Reynolds's death on August 12, 2000, there is no other expert in this area to consult.

12. See pages 297–301 of Paul Smith's *A Reader's Guide to the Short Stories of Ernest Hemingway* for the scant and unimpressive lineage of this short story.

13. On May 15, Hemingway would again note when he had accomplished some writing: "S.E. breeze—rained all day—did not go out—wrote (article) Pauline Karl went to bookstores—worked on title." On June 12, Hemingway would note, "worked all morning—finished story 24 pages." And on June 23, referring to himself in the third person, he recorded, "EH wrote 1500 words before going out." The time in Havana was considered a vacation. The writing projects Hemingway completed may have been the short stories "A Day's Wait" and/or "Fathers and Sons." Both short stories first appeared in the collection *Winner Take Nothing*, published on October 27, 1933. He also would have been working on the first draft of his initial article for *Esquire*, "Marlin Off the Morro: A Cuban Letter," which appeared in the first issue of the magazine, dated "Autumn, 1933."

14. This was the only reference to overdrinking I noted in the logs. Although in later years Hemingway became conclusively alcoholic, in 1933 he

could still be considered a heavy social drinker. In my opinion, alcoholism set in during 1942, as his marriage to Martha Gellhorn collapsed.

15. The superscripted minutes are a reproduction of Hemingway's short-hand notations for time. For 12:45 P.M., he would write "12" and then add the "45" in lowercase letters, underlined twice. Rather than misrepresent an element of punctuation that did not exist, I have decided to type the numbers without inserting the colon and superscript the minutes.

16. Nineteen arrobas is equal to 475 pounds.

17. Norberto Fuentes's book *Hemingway in Cuba* is more anecdotal than scholarly, and it is filled with inaccuracies. This description of so-called Hemingway's mile should be taken as a rough approximation.

18. According to *Webster's Ninth Collegiate Dictionary*, a mill race is a "canal in which water flows to and from a mill wheel" (755).

19. "Bumby" is the nickname of Hemingway's son John. He was the child from Hemingway's marriage to his first wife, Hadley Richardson. He would have been nine years old in May of 1933.

20. This passage from *The Old Man and the Sea* will be revisited in chapter 5.

21. Although the 1933 log continues through July 15, my discussion of it concludes with this examination of Hemingway's most complex entry.

22. Michael Reynolds paraphrases this poem of June 3, 1933, in *Hemingway: The 1930s* on pages 134–35. Yet his abridgement does not do justice to the entry, thus I quote it in full.

2. The Sea Change Part II

1. Hemingway named his boat *Pilar* in honor of the shrine and *feria* at Zaragoza, Spain, and also for his wife Pauline, who used "Pilar" as one of her secret nicknames when they first fell in love. See Baker, *Life* 259.

2. According to Megan Desnoyers, senior archivist at the John F. Kennedy Library, it is impossible to verify whether the language of the log is a direct transcription from Hemingway or Samuelson's approximation.

3. My examination of this log will be less exhaustive than the previous one since it was the subject of Linda Patterson Miller's wonderful article "The Matrix of Hemingway's *Pilar* Log, 1934–1935."

4. Since his marriage to Pauline Pfeiffer on May 10, 1927, Hemingway had been a practicing Roman Catholic. After their divorce on November 4, 1940, Hemingway's professions of religious faith became ambiguous, and his beliefs and practices need more scholarly attention. The best source on the subject is Larry Grimes's *The Religious Design of Hemingway's Early Fiction*.

5. The entire Donne epigraph reads: "No man is an *Illand*, intire of it selfe; every man is a peece of the *Continent*, a part of the *maine*; if a *Clod* bee

washed away by the *Sea, Europe* is the lesse, as well as if a *Promontorie* were, as well as if a *Mannor* of they friends or of *thine owne* were; any mans *death* diminishes *me*, because I am involved in *Mankinde*; And therefore never send to know for whom the *bell* tolls; It tolls for *thee*."

6. Samuelson is incorrect when he states that Hemingway initiated the correspondence. According to Larry Martin, it was in March 1934 that Hemingway received a "surprising letter from an American stranger," Cadwalader (5).

7. Since the carbon copy of the 1934 log was in the possession of the Samuelson family, it would seem likely that Hemingway retained the original to file with his other logs. Yet the original was not given to the John F. Kennedy Library with Hemingway's other papers. Ultimately, it is impossible to know whether Hemingway reviewed the 1934 log during the composition of *The Old Man and the Sea*.

8. According to Bruce Henderson of the Billfish Foundation, white, blue, black, and striped marlin are all distinct species. Although all black marlin are not females, they are characterized by sexual dimorphism, which means the females grow larger and stronger than males to ensure an ample supply of offspring to continue the species (Skorupa 44).

9. I am indebted to Gail Morchower, librarian at the International Game Fish Museum, for providing me with a copy of this article.

10. According to Lawrence Martin, "Hemingway frequently uses the common name 'black marlin' for a kind of Gulf Stream fish. Today the name 'black marlin' identifies a Pacific species" (14).

11. In 1935, 1936, and 1937, due to political turmoil in Cuba, Hemingway would spend more time fishing off the coast of Bimini than off the coast of Havana. For information on these years, see William Braasch Watson and Jane Day.

12. Perhaps revealing his pride in his own role, this article was kept by Hemingway in his fishing files that now reside in the Ernest Hemingway Collection at the John F. Kennedy Library.

13. According to Doug Blodgett, world records administrator of the International Game Fish Association, Hemingway at one time held records for the largest marlin caught off the Cuban coast (468 pounds; 1933) and the world record for bluefin tuna (381 pounds; 1935). He caught the third-largest mako shark (786 pounds) off the coast of Bimini in June 1935.

14. LaMonte was the author of four books on marine game fishes, including *Game Fish of the World*, which included an article on Cuban fishing by Hemingway. LaMonte's other titles were *North American Game Fishes* (1945), *A Review and Revision of the Marlins, Genus* Makiara (1955), and *Icthyological Contributions to the International Game Fish Association* (1941).

15. For more information on this trip and Clapp's catch, see my "Hemingway's Hawaiian Honeymoon."

3. Hemingway's Aesthetics

1. Critical theory has contested the aesthetic of realism and literary naturalism, stressing that "reality" is created rather than discovered. Since the focus
of this section is on interpretations of Hemingway's style and philosophy, that
debate and conversation cannot be explored in full. For an overview of recent de-
velopments in this field, see David E. Shi's *Facing Facts: Realism in American
Thought and Culture, 1850–1920*, 374. According to Christophe Den Tandt,

> The reappraisal of the realist and naturalist corpus in the last fifteen years
> has shattered the belief that novels can reveal the truth of the social world
> merely by offering snapshots of urban poverty. Critics like Rachel Bowlby,
> June Howard, Amy Kaplan, Walter Benn Michaels, and Mark Seltzer have
> discarded the theory of literary mimesis that takes for granted that social
> facts can be represented by means of a transparent documentary aesthetic.
> In the process, the realist and naturalist city, no longer a mere setting for
> positivistic surveys, has become an intricate field of power relationships
> structured by interrelated discourses of economic production, population
> management, and racial and gender definition. (ix)

2. I am indebted to Joseph Stanton for clarifying this aspect of Hemingway's artistic affinities.

3. To assist the reader in understanding the time elapsed between
events, and their subsequent appearance in published fiction, a chronology is
provided as Appendix A.

4. Literary Naturalism on the Stream

1. Toni Morrison considers Morgan a surrogate for Hemingway. In her
1992 book *Playing in the Dark: Whiteness and the Literary Imagination*, she
wrote:

> My interest in Ernest Hemingway becomes heightened when I consider
> how much apart his work is from African-Americans. That is, he has no
> need, desire, or awareness of them either as readers of his work, or as
> people existing anywhere other than in his imaginative (an imaginatively
> lived) world. I find, therefore, his use of African-Americans much more
> artless and unselfconscious than Poe's, for example, where social unease
> required the servile black bodies in his work. Hemingway's work could be
> described as innocent of nineteenth-century ideological agenda as well as
> free of what may be called recent, postmodernist sensitivity. (69–70)

2. Toni Knott writes of *To Have and Have Not:* "Hemingway meticu-
lously chose exact characteristics to best capture the category represented by

that individual to illustrate that the only way to transcend stereotyping is to take the time to know the individual" (86).

3. Bert Bender argues that Darwin's ideas were not important to Hemingway. Bender writes:

> It is important to remember that during the years when Hemingway became a writer, Darwin's ideas were passe. . . . But in the early stages of Hemingway's career, the disillusionment caused by World War I, the possibility of a Marxist solution to social injustice, the Waste Land view of modern life, the intensifying interest in Freud and Jung (both were heavily influenced by Darwinian thought), and the beginnings of New Critical thought in the aesthetics of Ezra Pound and T. S. Eliot: these were the prevailing currents of American literary thought. (170)

4. Evidence countering Bert Bender's assertion of Darwin's unimportance to Hemingway exists in that the Finca Vigia's library included *Charles Darwin and the Voyage of the Beagle: Unpublished Letters and Notebooks*, edited by Nora Barlow (New York: Philosophical Library, 1946), and *The Darwin Reader*, edited by Marston Bates and Philip S. Humphrey (New York: Scribners, 1956). See Brasch and Sigman, 93.

5. The language is parallel to the phrasing he used in his letter to Mrs. Paul Pfeiffer, quoted earlier in this chapter: "I am trying to make, before I get through, a picture of the whole world—or as much of it as I have seen. Boiling it down always, rather than spreading it thin" (*Selected Letters* 397).

6. Hemingway would write, "Marx the whimpering bourgeois living on the bounty of Engels is exactly as valid as Dos Passos living on a yacht in the Mediterranean while he attacks the capitalist system." The reference is to Dos Passos's visit with the Murphy family in the summer of 1933, when he was recovering from a severe attack of rheumatic fever (see Baker, *Life* 612).

7. With the publication of *To Have and Have Not*, Hemingway would appear on the cover of *Time* on October 18, 1937.

8. Hemingway finished writing *To Have and Have Not* on January 2, 1937. It would be published on October 15, 1937.

9. These same critics overlook the importance of his script for the Joris Ivens film *The Spanish Earth*, screened by the Roosevelts at the White House with the Hemingways as guests on July 8, 1937. Another public declaration of his complex political sympathies was the publication of his article "Who Murdered the Vets?" in *The New Masses*, on September 17, 1935.

10. According to Leon Edel, "Ernest Hemingway was the creator of the legend that Henry James was impotent. . . . The novelist . . . developed this fantasy from Van Wyck Brooks's *The Pilgrimage of Henry James* (1925) which

appeared while he was writing his novel (*The Sun Also Rises*)" (721–22). For more on Hemingway and James, see Peter Hays.

11. Saul Bellow wrote: "Hemingway is a glamorous person; his art and wounds make him respected; his vanity and his peculiar attributes provoke envy and anger; his fans are often maddening and his detractors include some of the prize goops of our troubled time. . . . Clearly Hemingway, whether we like it or not, has found some of the secret places of our pride and trouble" (18).

12. See Michael Reynolds's *Hemingway's Reading, 1910–1940: An Inventory* for a list of books that Hemingway read at Oak Park High School. Brasch and Sigman's *Hemingway's Library: A Composite Record* is a record of books that Hemingway owned, not necessarily that he read.

13. *Green Hills of Africa* was published on October 25, 1935. "The Snows of Kilimanjaro" would be published in *Esquire* in August 1936, and "The Short Happy Life of Francis Macomber" would be published in *Esquire* the following month, September 1936.

5. ILLUSTRATING THE ICEBERG

1. My footnote in "Hemingway's Hawaiian Honeymoon" that summarizes this inquiry reads: "Michael Culver asserts that the story is founded upon a combination of commercial fisherman Carlos Gutierrez's experience and the actual events of the Strater-Hemingway Bimini trip of 1935" (31). Dos Passos suggests that a shark attack on a tuna Hemingway caught near Bimini in 1934 provided the impetus for the story (60–67). Rose Marie Burwell claims that Hemingway found inspiration for the marlin off Bimini in 1936 (61). Dos Passos's dates are clearly in error, as Hemingway was not in Bimini until 1935, which was the only time Dos Passos joined him there.

2. In that article, Hemingway wrote:

Another time an old man fishing alone in a skiff out of Cabanas hooked a great marlin that, on the heavy sashcord handline, pulled the skiff far out to sea. Two days later the old man was picked up by fishermen sixty miles to the westward, the head and forward part of the marlin lashed alongside. What was left of the fish, less than half, weighed 800 pounds. The old man had stayed with him a day, a night, a day and another night while the fish swam deep and pulled the boat. When he had come up the old man had pulled the boat up on him and harpooned him. Lashed alongside the sharks had hit him and the old man had fought them out alone in the Gulf Stream in a skiff, clubbing them, stabbing at them, lunging at them with an oar until he was exhausted and the sharks had eaten all that they could hold. He was crying in the boat when the fishermen picked him up, half crazy from his loss, and the sharks were still circling the boat. ("On the Blue Water" 230–31)

3. The trip, which included famous sportsmen of the era Phillip Percival, Alfred Vanderbilt, and Baron von Blixen, was unexpectedly successful. The party caught kingfish, amberjacks, dolphins, and sailfish (see Baker, *Life* 257).

4. In famous interviews with Lillian Ross in 1952, and in 1958 with George Plimpton, Hemingway again remarked on his debt to Cézanne. To Ross, he said: "I can make a landscape like Mr. Paul Cezanne [*sic*]. I learned how to make a landscape by walking through the Luxembourg Museum a thousand times with an empty gut, and I am pretty sure that if Mr. Paul was around he would like the way I make them and be happy I learned from him" (60). To Plimpton, Hemingway lists Cézanne as a "writer" he has learned from, pronouncing: "I put in painters because I learned as much from painters about how to write as from writers" (118). In *A Moveable Feast* (1964), which he began writing in 1957, Hemingway states: "I was learning something from the painting of Cezanne that made writing simple true sentences far from enough to make the stories have the dimensions I was trying to put in. I was not articulate enough to explain it to anyone. Besides it was a secret" (13).

5. According to Allen Josephs, James Michener is a writer who would best illustrate the opposite of the iceberg principle (54).

6. Since Linda Patterson Miller examines the whale incident in her article, I do not explore it further here. See "The Matrix of Hemingway's *Pilar* Log, 1934–1935," 112–13. In the *Esquire* article, Hemingway wrote:

As we looked astern to the eastward, there were spouts rising almost as far as you could see. It looked like a small geyser basin in Yellowstone Park. There were at least ten whales blowing at once and while we watched more than twenty showed; some close, some far out, some far to the east. Some spouts were high thin plumes spreading on top. Others were low, squat, wide. ("There She Breaches!" 241)

7. The interview is transcribed in full in chapter 1.

8. Although he did write journalism, Hemingway published no fiction in the years from 1941 to 1951. Much of 1941 was lost to travel to Hawaii, China, and the Philippines (February 11 to May 6). From July 1942 to September 1943, Hemingway used the *Pilar* to hunt submarines in the Caribbean. They never encountered an enemy vessel. From May 17, 1944, to March 6, 1945, Hemingway was in Europe covering and participating in World War II. In January 1946, Hemingway began writing a novel set in the French Riviera, the urtext that would generate *The Old Man and the Sea*, along with other

works. Because of this stunning absence of imaginative activity, I would place the onset of Hemingway's alcoholism in July 1942, when Martha Gellhorn, his third wife, left Cuba to resume her career and his drink-soaked submarine patrols begin.

Appendix A

The dates for my chronology are taken from Michael Reynolds's *Hemingway: The 1930s*, Rose Marie Burwell's *Hemingway: The Postwar Years and the Posthumous Novels*, Robert Trogdon's *Ernest Hemingway: A Literary Reference*, and Carlos Baker's *Hemingway: A Life Story*, as well as the fishing logs at the John F. Kennedy Library in Boston.

Works Consulted

Attebery, Brian. "American Studies: A Not So Unscientific Method." *American Quarterly* 48 (June 1996): 316–43.

Baker, Carlos. *Hemingway: A Life Story*. New York: Scribners, 1969.

———. *Hemingway: The Writer as Artist*. 1952. Princeton, NJ: Princeton University Press, 1990.

———. "Hemingway's Ancient Mariner." *Ernest Hemingway: Critiques of Four Major Novels*. Ed. Carlos Baker. New York: Scribners, 1962. 161–72.

Beegel, Susan F. "Eye and Heart: Hemingway's Education as a Naturalist." *A Historical Guide to Ernest Hemingway*. Ed. Linda Wagner-Martin. New York: Oxford University Press, 2000. 53–92.

Bellow, Saul. "Hemingway and the Image of Man." *Partisan Review* June–July 1953: 18.

Bender, Bert. *Sea-Brothers: The Tradition of American Sea Fiction from "Moby-Dick" to the Present*. Philadelphia: University of Pennsylvania Press, 1988.

Bercovitch, Sacvan, ed. *Reconstructing American Literary History*. Cambridge, MA: Harvard University Press, 1986.

Blodgett, Doug. E-mail to the author. December 3, 2001.

Boime, Albert. "Blacks in Shark-Infested Waters: Visual Encodings of Racism in Copley and Homer." *Smithsonian Studies in American Art* 3 (Winter 1989): 19–47.

Brasch, James D. E-mail to the author. January 12, 2002.

Brasch, James D., and Joseph Sigman. *Hemingway's Library: A Composite Record*. New York: Garland, 1981.

Brooks, Van Wycks. "On Creating a Usable Past." *The Dial* April 11, 1918: 337–41.

Bruccoli, Matthew J., ed. *Conversations with Ernest Hemingway*. Jackson: University Press of Mississippi, 1986.

Burhans, Clinton S. "*The Old Man and the Sea*: Hemingway's Tragic Vision of Man." *Ernest Hemingway: Critiques of Four Major Novels*. Ed. Carlos Baker. New York: Scribners, 1962. 150–55.

Burwell, Rose Marie. *Hemingway: The Postwar Years and the Posthumous Novels*. New York: Cambridge University Press, 1996.

Busch, Frederick. "Reading Hemingway Without Guilt." *New York Times Book Review* January 12, 1992: 1, 17–19.

Byrne, Janice F. "New Acquisitions Shed Light on 'The Old Man and the Sea.'" *Hemingway Review* 10.2 (Spring 1991): 68–70.

Cadwalader, Charles M. B. Letters to Ernest Hemingway. 1934–35. Incoming Correspondence. The Hemingway Collection. John F. Kennedy Library, Boston.

Carson, Rachel. *The Sea Around Us*. Oxford: Oxford University Press, 1951.

Chase, Richard. *The American Novel and Its Tradition*. Baltimore, MD: Johns Hopkins University Press, 1957.

———, ed. *Melville: A Collection of Critical Essays*. Englewood Cliffs, NJ: Prentice-Hall, 1962.

Chowder, Ken. "Winslow Homer, the Quintessential American Artist." *Smithsonian* October 1995: 116–29.

Civello, Paul. *American Literary Naturalism and Its Twentieth-Century Transformations: Frank Norris, Ernest Hemingway, Don DeLillo*. Athens: University of Georgia Press, 1994.

Conder, John J. *Naturalism in American Fiction: The Classic Phase*. Lexington: University of Kentucky Press, 1984.

Cooper, Helen A. *Winslow Homer Watercolors*. New Haven, CT: Yale University Press, 1986.

Crane, Stephen. "The Open Boat." *Great Short Works of Stephen Crane*. New York: Harper and Row, 1965. 277–302.

Culver, Michael. "Sparring in the Dark: Hemingway, Strater, and 'The Old Man and the Sea.'" *Hemingway Review* 11.2 (Spring 1992): 31–37.

Dana, Richard Henry. *Two Years Before the Mast*. Herefordshire, UK: Wordsworth Classics, 1996.

Day, Jane. "Hemingway in Bimini." *South Florida History* Fall 1989: 5–9, 24.

DeFalco, Joseph. "'Bimini' and the Subject of Hemingway's *Islands in the Stream*." *Ernest Hemingway: Six Decades of Criticism*. Ed. Linda W. Wagner. East Lansing: Michigan State University Press, 1987. 313–24.

Delbanco, Andrew. "The Decline and Fall of Literature." *New York Review of Books* November 4, 1999: 32–38.

————. *Required Reading: Why Our American Classics Matter Now*. New York: Farrar, Straus and Giroux, 1997.

Den Tandt, Christophe. *The Urban Sublime in American Literary Naturalism*. Urbana: University of Illinois Press, 1998.

Donaldson, Scott. *Force of Will: The Life and Art of Ernest Hemingway*. New York: Viking, 1977.

Dos Passos, John. "Old Hem Was a Sport." *Sports Illustrated* June 29, 1964: 60–67.

Downes, William Howe. *The Life and Work of Winslow Homer*. 1911. New York: Dover, 1989.

Edel, Leon. *Henry James: A Life*. New York: Harper and Row, 1985.

Farrington, S. Kip. *Atlantic Big Game Fishing*. New York: Kennedy Bros., 1937.

Fenstermaker, John J. "Hemingway and the Gulf Stream: The *Esquire* Letters as Informal Apologia." *Studies in American Culture* 20.2 (October 1997): 41–57.

Fielder, Leslie. *Love and Death in the American Novel*. New York: Anchor Books, 1992.

Flexner, James Thomas. *The World of Winslow Homer: 1836–1910*. New York: Time, Inc., 1971.

Fowler, Henry W. "Description of a New Scorpaenoid Fish (*Neomerinthe Hemingwayi*) from Off New Jersey." *Proceedings of the Academy of Natural Sciences of Philadelphia* 87 (1935): 41–43.

————. Letter to Ernest Hemingway. August 8, 1935. Incoming Correspondence. The Hemingway Collection. John F. Kennedy Library, Boston.

Frank, Stuart M. *Herman Melville's Picture Gallery: Sources and Types of the "Pictorial" Chapters of "Moby-Dick."* Fairhaven, MA: Edward Lefkowicz, 1986.

Fuentes, Norberto. *Hemingway in Cuba*. Secaucus, NJ: Lyle Stuart, 1984.

Funcia, Claudio Izquierdo. *Hemingway: Poor Old Papa*. Havana: Ediciones Mec-Graphic, 1995.

Gajdusek, Robin. "Hemingway's Late-Life Relationship with Birds." *Hemingway and the Natural World*. Ed. Robert E. Fleming. Moscow: University of Idaho Press, 1999. 175–87.

Gendin, Sidney. "Was Stephen Crane (or Anybody Else) a Naturalist?" *Cambridge Quarterly* 24.2 (1995): 89–101.

Gingrich, Arnold. "Publisher's Page: Notes on 'Bimini.'" *Esquire* October 1970: 6.

Goadby, Peter. *Saltwater Gamefishing: Offshore and Onshore*. Sydney, Australia: Angus & Robertson, 1991.

Greenfield, George. "Wood Field and Stream." *New York Times* May 13, 1935.

Grimes, Larry. *The Religious Design of Hemingway's Early Fiction.* Ann Arbor, MI: UMI Research Press, 1985.

Hart, James D. *The Concise Oxford Companion to American Literature.* Oxford: Oxford University Press, 1988.

Hays, Peter. "Hemingway's *The Sun Also Rises* and James's *The Ambassadors.*" *Hemingway Review* 20.2 (Spring 2001): 90–98.

Hemingway, Ernest. "After the Storm." *The Short Stories of Ernest Hemingway.* New York: Scribners, 1938. 372–78.

———. "Che Ti Dice La Patria?" Manuscript Folder 727. The Hemingway Collection. John F. Kennedy Library, Boston.

———. "Cuban Fishing." *Game Fish of the World.* Ed. Brian Vesey-Fitzgerald and Francesca LaMonte. London: Nicholson & Watson, 1949. 156–60.

———. *Death in the Afternoon.* New York: Scribners, 1932.

———. *Ernest Hemingway: Selected Letters, 1917–1961.* Ed. Carlos Baker. New York: Scribners, 1981.

———. *A Farewell to Arms.* New York: Scribners, 1929.

———. Fishing Log. June 7–20, 1932. Box 88. The Hemingway Collection. John F. Kennedy Library, Boston.

———. Fishing Log. January 25–May 15, 1933. Box 88. The Hemingway Collection. John F. Kennedy Library, Boston.

———. Fishing Log. July 28, 1934–February 2, 1935. Box 88. The Hemingway Collection. John F. Kennedy Library, Boston.

———. *For Whom the Bell Tolls.* New York: Scribners, 1940.

———. *Green Hills of Africa.* New York: Scribners, 1935.

———. "He Who Gets Slap Happy: A Bimini Letter." *Esquire* August 1935: 21, 174.

———. *Hemingway on Fishing.* Ed. Nick Lyons. New York: Lyons Press, 2000.

———. *Hemingway on War.* Ed. Seán Hemingway. New York: Scribners, 2003.

———. *In Our Time.* New York: Scribners, 1925.

———. Introduction. *Atlantic Game Fishing.* By S. Kip Farrington Jr. Lyon, MS: Derrydale, 1937.

———. Introduction. *A Farewell to Arms.* New York: Scribners, 1948. vii–xi.

———. *Islands in the Stream.* New York: Scribners, 1970.

———. Letter to Francesca LaMonte. July 18, 1941. The Hemingway Collection. John F. Kennedy Library, Boston.

———. Log of the *Pilar.* 1934–35. The Hemingway Collection. John F. Kennedy Library, Boston.

———. "Marlin Off Cuba." In *American Big Game Fishing.* Ed. Eugene V.

Connett. Lyon, MS: Derrydale, 1993. 55–81. Facsimile reprint of the 1935 edition.

———. "Marlin Off the Morro: A Cuban Letter." *By-line: Ernest Hemingway.* Ed. William White. New York: Scribners, 1967. 138–44.

———. *A Moveable Feast.* New York: Scribners, 1964.

———. *The Nick Adams Stories.* New York: Scribners, 1972.

———. *The Old Man and the Sea.* New York: Scribners, 1952.

———. *The Only Thing That Counts: The Ernest Hemingway–Maxwell Perkins Correspondence.* Ed. Matthew Bruccoli. New York: Scribners, 1996.

———. "On the Blue Water: A Gulf Stream Letter." *By-line: Ernest Hemingway.* Ed. William White. New York: Scribners, 1967. 236–44.

———. "On Writing." *The Nick Adams Stories.* New York: Scribners, 1972. 233–41.

———. "Out in the Stream: A Cuban Letter." *By-line: Ernest Hemingway.* Ed. William White. New York: Scribners, 1967. 169–75.

———. "There She Breaches! Or Moby Dick Off the Morro." *By-line: Ernest Hemingway.* Ed. William White. New York: Scribners, 1967. 245–54.

———. *To Have and Have Not.* New York: Scribners, 1937.

Hemingway, Leicester. *My Brother, Ernest Hemingway.* Greenwich, CT: Fawcett, 1961.

Hemingway, Mary Welsh. *How It Was.* New York: Alfred A. Knopf, 1976.

A History of the IGFA. Fort Lauderdale, FL: International Game Fishing Association, 1991.

Hoopes, Donelson F. *Winslow Homer Watercolors.* New York: Watson-Guptill, 1969.

Horowitz, Richard. "Teaching About Method." *American Quarterly* 31.1 (Spring 1990): 101–16.

Josephs, Allen. "How Did Hemingway Write?" *North Dakota Quarterly* 63.3 (Summer 1996): 50–64.

Kael, Pauline. "Stag Show." *New Yorker* March 14, 1971: 125.

Karcher, Carolyn L. *Shadow Over the Promised Land: Slavery, Race, and Violence in Melville's America.* Baton Rouge: Louisiana State University Press, 1980.

Kazin, Alfred. *An American Procession: The Major American Writers from 1830–1930—the Crucial Century.* New York: Random House, 1984.

———. "Hemingway the Painter." *New Republic* March 19, 1977: 21–28.

———. *On Native Grounds: An Interpretation of Modern American Prose Literature.* New York: Harcourt Brace, 1995.

Kelly, Franklin. "Time and Narrative Erased." *Winslow Homer.* Ed. Nicolai Cikovsky and Franklin Kelly. New Haven, CT: Yale University Press, 1995. 300–15.

Knott, Toni D. "Playing in the Light: Examining Categorization in *To Have and Have Not* as a Reflection of Identity or Racism." *North Dakota Quarterly* 64.3 (Fall 1997): 82–88.

Kolodny, Annette. *The Lay of the Land: Metaphor as Experience in American Life and Letters.* Chapel Hill: University of North Carolina Press, 1975.

Kuklick, Bruce. "Myth and Symbol in American Studies." *American Quarterly* 24 (1972): 435–50.

Lair, Robert L. "Hemingway and Cézanne: An Indebtedness." *Modern Fiction Studies* 6 (1960): 165–68.

Lauter, Paul. *Canons and Contexts.* New York: Oxford University Press, 1991.

Limerick, Patricia Nelson. *The Legacy of Conquest: The Unbroken Past of the American West.* New York: W. W. Norton, 1987.

Little, Carl. *Winslow Homer and the Sea.* San Francisco: Pomegranate Art Books, 1995.

Lynn, Kenneth. *Hemingway.* New York: Fawcett Columbine, 1987.

Mandel, Miriam. *Reading Hemingway: The Facts in the Fictions.* Metuchen, NJ: Scarecrow Press, 1995.

Martin, Lawrence H. "Ernest Hemingway, Gulf Stream Marine Scientist: The 1934–35 Academy of Natural Sciences Correspondence." *Hemingway Review* 20.2 (Spring 2001): 5–15.

Marx, Leo. *The Machine in the Garden: Technology and the Pastoral Ideal in America. New York.* New York: Oxford University Press, 1967.

———. "Pastoralism in America." *Ideology and Classic American Literature.* Ed. Sacvan Bercovitch and Myra Jehlen. New York: Cambridge University Press, 1986. 36–70.

Mathewson, Stephen. "Against the Stream: Thomas Hudson and Painting." *North Dakota Quarterly* 57.4 (1989): 140–45.

Matthiessen, F. O. *American Renaissance: Art and Expression in the Age of Whitman and Emerson.* London: Oxford University Press, 1941.

McCormick, John. *American and European Literary Imagination, 1919–1932.* 1971. New Brunswick, NJ: Transaction Publishers, 2000.

McKay, Claude. "On Hemingway." *A Long Way From Home.* New York: Lee Furman, 1937. 249–52.

McLendon, James. *Papa: Hemingway in Key West, 1928–1940.* New York: Popular Library, 1972.

Mellow, James R. *Hemingway: A Life Without Consequences.* New York: Houghton Mifflin, 1992.

Melville, Herman. *Moby-Dick.* New York: Bantam Books, 1986.

———. *Redburn: His First Voyage.* Evanston, IL: Northwestern University Press and the Newberry Library, 1969.

———. *Typee.* Herefordshire, UK: Wordsworth Classics, 1994.

Meyers, Jeffrey. *Hemingway: A Biography.* New York: Harper and Row, 1985.

Miller, Linda Patterson. "The Matrix of Hemingway's *Pilar* Log, 1934–1935." *North Dakota Quarterly* 64.3 (Fall 1997): 105–23.

Montenegro, David. "An Interview with Derek Walcott." *Conversations with Derek Walcott.* Ed. William Baer. Jackson: University Press of Mississippi, 1996. 135–50.

Morrison, Toni. *Playing in the Dark: Whiteness and the Literary Imagination.* New York: Random House, 1992.

Mumford, Lewis. *Herman Melville.* New York: Harcourt Brace, 1929.

Murphy, Charlene M. "Hemingway, Winslow Homer, and *Islands in the Stream:* Influence and Tribute." *Hemingway Review* 13.1 (Fall 1993): 76–85.

———. "Hemingway's Gentle Hunters: Contradiction or Duality?" *Hemingway and the Natural World.* Ed. Robert E. Fleming. Moscow: University of Idaho Press, 1999. 165–74.

Nanny, Max. "Hemingway's Architecture of Prose: Chiastic Patterns and Their Narrative Functions." *North Dakota Quarterly* 64.3 (1997): 157–76.

Nelson, Raymond S. *Hemingway: Expressionist Artist.* Ames: Iowa State University Press, 1979.

Novak, Barbara. *American Painting of the Nineteenth Century: Realism, Idealism, and the American Experience.* New York: Harper and Row, 1969.

O'Brine, Jack. "Highly Praised By Hemingway." *Havana Post* October 26, 1934.

Ott, Mark P. "Hemingway's Hawaiian Honeymoon." *Hemingway Review* 17.1 (Fall 1997): 58–67.

Paul, Steve. "On Hemingway and His Influence." *Hemingway Review* 18.2 (1999): 115–32.

Philbrick, Nathaniel. *American Sea Writing: A Literary Anthology.* New York: Library of America, 2000.

Pizer, Donald. *The Theory and Practice of American Literary Naturalism: Selected Essays and Reviews.* Carbondale: Southern Illinois University Press, 1983.

Plimpton, George. "Ernest Hemingway. An Interview." *Paris Review* Spring 1958: 61–89.

"Prowess in Action." *Time* July 24, 1935: 24.

Reiger, George. *Profiles in Saltwater Angling: A History of the Sport—Its People and Places, Tackle and Techniques.* Englewood Cliffs, NJ: Prentice-Hall, 1973.

Renker, Elizabeth. *Strike Through the Mask: Herman Melville and the Scene of Writing.* Baltimore, MD: Johns Hopkins University Press, 1996.

Reynolds, Michael. *Hemingway: The American Homecoming.* London: Basil Blackwell, 1992.

———. *Hemingway: The Final Years.* New York: W. W. Norton, 1999.

———. *Hemingway: The 1930s.* New York: W. W. Norton, 1997.

———. *Hemingway: The Paris Years.* London: Basil Blackwell, 1989.

———. *Hemingway's Reading, 1910–1940: An Inventory.* Princeton, NJ: Princeton University Press, 1981.

———. *The Young Hemingway.* London: Basil Blackwell, 1986.

Robertson-Lorant, Laurie. *Melville: A Biography.* New York: Clarkson Potter, 1996.

Roman, Erl. "Angler Notes." *Miami Herald* May 23, 1935.

———. "Angler Notes." *Miami Herald* June 22, 1935.

Ross, Lillian. *Portrait of Hemingway: The Celebrated Profile.* 1950. New York: Avon Library, 1961.

Rowe, Anne E. *The Idea of Florida in the American Literary Imagination.* Gainesville: University Press of Florida, 1992.

Samuelson, Arnold. *With Hemingway: A Year in Key West and Cuba.* New York: Holt, Rinehart and Winston, 1984.

Schama, Simon. "Homer's Odyssey: What Drove Winslow Homer to the Sea?" *New Yorker* October 17, 1997: 60–63.

Schnitzer, Deborah. *The Pictorial in Modernist Fiction: From Stephen Crane to Ernest Hemingway.* Ann Arbor, MI: UMI Research Press, 1988.

Sealts, Merton M. *Melville's Reading: Revised and Enlarged Edition.* Rev. ed. Columbia: University of South Carolina Press, 1988.

Shi, David E. *Facing Facts: Realism in American Thought and Culture, 1850–1920.* New York: Oxford University Press, 1995.

Shumway, David R. *Creating American Civilization: A Genealogy of American Literature as an American Discipline.* Minneapolis: University of Minnesota Press, 1994.

Singal, Daniel. *William Faulkner: The Making of a Modernist.* Chapel Hill: University of North Carolina Press, 1997.

Skorupa, Joe. "Debunking Hemingway's Marlin Theories." *Popular Mechanics* October 1989: 44.

Slotkin, Richard. "Myth and the Production of History." *Ideology and Classic American Literature.* Ed. Sacvan Bercovitch and Myra Jehlen. Cambridge: Cambridge University Press, 1986. 70–90.

Smith, Henry Nash. *Virgin Land: The American West as Symbol and Myth.* Cambridge, MA: Harvard University Press, 1950.

Smith, Paul. *A Reader's Guide to the Short Stories of Ernest Hemingway.* Boston: G. K. Hall, 1989.

Stephens, Robert O. *Hemingway's Nonfiction: The Public Voice.* Chapel Hill: University of North Carolina Press, 1968.

Sundquist, Eric J., ed. *American Realism: New Essays.* Baltimore, MD: Johns Hopkins University Press, 1982.

Susman, Warren. *Culture as History: The Transformation of American Society in the Twentieth Century.* New York: Pantheon, 1984.

Sylvester, Bickford. "The Cuban Context of *The Old Man and the Sea.*" *The Cambridge Companion to Ernest Hemingway.* Ed. Scott Donaldson. Cambridge: Cambridge University Press, 1996. 243–68.

———. "Hemingway's Extended Vision: *The Old Man and the Sea.*" *Twentieth Century Interpretations of* The Old Man and the Sea: *A Collection of Critical Essays.* Ed. Katharine T. Jobes. Englewood Cliffs, NJ: Prentice-Hall, 1968. 81–96.

Tompkins, Jane. *West of Everything: The Inner Life of Westerns.* New York: Oxford University Press, 1992.

Trachtenberg, Alan. "American Studies as a Cultural Program." *Ideology and Classic American Literature.* Ed. Sacvan Bercovitch and Myra Jehlen. Cambridge: Cambridge University Press, 1986. 172–87.

———. *Brooklyn Bridge: Fact and Symbol.* Chicago: University of Chicago Press, 1965.

Trogdon, Robert W. *Ernest Hemingway: A Literary Reference.* New York: Carroll & Graf, 1999.

Trullinger, Ray. "New Big Fish Club Is Organized, But It's Awfully Hard to Crash." *New York City World Telegram* November 23, 1936.

Updike, John. "Melville's Withdrawal." *Hugging the Shore: Essays and Criticism.* New York: Random House, 1983. 80–106.

———. "The Sinister Sex." *Odd Jobs: Essays and Criticism.* New York: Alfred A. Knopf, 1991.

Voss, Frederick. *Picturing Hemingway: A Writer in His Time.* New Haven, CT: Yale University Press, 1999.

Walcott, Derek. *Collected Poems: 1948–1984.* New York: Farrar, Straus and Giroux, 1986.

———. "Hemingway as Poet." The Canon Before and After Hemingway (Plenary Session). Hemingway Centennial at the Kennedy Library, Boston. April 11, 1999.

———. "The Muse of History." *What the Twilight Says: Essays.* New York: Farrar, Straus and Giroux, 1998. 36–64.

———. *Omeros.* New York: Farrar, Straus and Giroux, 1990.

———. "On Hemingway." *What the Twilight Says: Essays.* New York: Farrar, Straus and Giroux, 1998. 106–18.

Walcutt, Charles Child. *American Literary Naturalism, A Divided Stream.* Minneapolis: University of Minnesota Press, 1956.

Waldmeir, Joseph. "Confiteor Hominem: Ernest Hemingway's Religion of Man." *Hemingway: A Collection of Critical Essays*. Ed. Robert P. Weeks. Englewood Cliffs, NJ: Prentice-Hall, 1962. 161–71.

Watson, William Braasch. "Hemingway in Bimini: An Introduction." *North Dakota Quarterly* 63.3 (Summer 1996): 130–44.

Watts, Emily. *Ernest Hemingway and the Arts*. Urbana: University of Illinois Press, 1971.

Weatherford, Richard M., ed. *Stephen Crane: The Critical Heritage*. London: Routledge & Kegan Paul, 1973.

Weeks, Robert P. "Fakery in *The Old Man and the Sea*." *Twentieth Century Interpretations of* The Old Man and the Sea. Ed. Katharine T. Jobes. *Hemingway: A Collection of Critical Essays*. Ed. Robert P. Weeks. Englewood Cliffs, NJ: Prentice-Hall, 1962. 34–40.

Wertheim, Stanley. *A Stephen Crane Encyclopedia*. Westport, CT: Greenwood Press, 1997.

Wertheim, Stanley, and Paul Sorrentino, eds. *The Crane Log: A Documentary Life of Stephen Crane, 1871–1900*. New York: Macmillan, 1992.

West, Ray B. "The Biological Trap." *Hemingway: A Collection of Critical Essays*. Ed. Robert P. Weeks. Englewood Cliffs, NJ: Prentice-Hall, 1962. 139–51.

Williams, Terry Tempest. "Hemingway and the Natural World." Keynote Address, Seventh International Hemingway Conference, Ketchum, ID. July 20, 1996.

Wilmerding, John. *American Marine Painting*. New York: Henry N. Abrams, 1968.

———. *American Views: Essays on American Art*. Princeton, NJ: Princeton University Press, 1991.

———. *Winslow Homer*. New York: Praeger, 1972,

Wilson, Edmund. "An Effort at Self-Revelation." Rev. of *Islands in the Stream* by Ernest Hemingway. *New Yorker* January 2, 1971: 61.

———. "The Sportsman's Tragedy." *The Shores of Light: A Literary Chronicle of the 1920s and 1930s*. 1927. Boston: Northeastern University Press, 1985.

Wise, Gene. "'Paradigm Dramas' in American Studies: A Cultural and Institutional History of the Movement." *American Quarterly* 31.3 (1979): 293–337.

Wolford, Chester L. *The Anger of Stephen Crane: Fiction and the Epic Tradition*. Lincoln: University of Nebraska Press, 1983.

Wood, Peter H. "Waiting in Limbo: A Reconsideration of Winslow Homer's *The Gulf Stream*." *The Southern Enigma: Essays in Race, Class, and*

Folk Culture. Ed. Walter J. Fraser and Winfred B. Moore Jr. Westport, CT: Greenwood Press, 1983. 76–95.

Wood, Peter H., and Karen C. C. Dalton. *Winslow Homer's Images of Blacks: The Civil War and Reconstruction Years.* Austin: University of Texas Press, 1988.

Young, Philip. *Ernest Hemingway: A Reconsideration.* 1952. New York: Harcourt, Brace & World, 1966.

Ziff, Larzer. *Literary Democracy: The Declaration of Cultural Independence in America.* New York: Penguin Books, 1981.

Index

feelings about, 19, 79–80; influences on, 46, 131n4; intellectual life in, 85–86; methods for, 89; need for expertise in, 98–99; quantity of, 20–21, 89, 125n13; sources for, 83–84, 86–87

Writing style, Hemingway's: descriptions in, 58–59, 69, 109; of *Esquire* articles, 18, 48–51; in fishing logs, 21–22, 24–26, 30, 32–34, 39–41, 124n4; goals for, 2, 66–67, 82, 129n5; Hemingway comparing own to others', 79, 100; Hemingway's description of, 64, 72; influences on, 65–66, 68–69, 81–82; language of, 44–45, 64, 98–99; as letters, 48–51; of *The Old Man and the Sea,* 89, 97–98, 101–2, 105; as painting with words, 2, 35, 59, 65, 67–69, 98–99, 108–9; realism in, 106, 109; as realist, modernist, and naturalist, 58–59; strengths in, 125n9; techniques in, 35, 62, 78; of *To Have and Have Not,* 97–98; transformations in, 7, 34–35, 44–45, 53, 58–59, 64, 70, 81–82, 97–99, 105–6. *See also* "Iceberg principle"

Wyoming, 17

Young, Philip, 82–83